In this thoroughly revised edition of *Surprised by* ~~~~~~~~~~~~~
Jack Deere has provided the body of Christ with the most biblical
and practical treatment available on this crucial topic. I know of no
one else in the church who is as well grounded in the Scriptures
and skilled in the practical dynamics of prophetic ministry as Jack
Deere. If you have ever been told that the revelatory gifts of the
Spirit are a threat to the Bible's sufficiency for life and godliness,
this is the book for you. Simply put, this is the book for all of us!
I can't recommend it too highly.

Sam Storms, PhD, Enjoying God Ministries

From the opening sentence, Jack Deere grabs your heart and mind
with a compelling mixture of biblical insight, stories, personal testimony, church history, and godly wisdom. This book is a tremendous
read! Whatever your experience has been, your faith will be built up,
your mind stimulated, and your spirit stirred with a greater desire
to hear the voice of God ever more clearly.

Hannah and Alex Absalom,
leaders of Dandelion Resourcing, and authors of
Hearing the Voice of God and *Healing the Sick*

Jack Deere has done it again! In this all-new, updated edition of
his classic on hearing the voice of God, he reminds us that God
never stopped speaking to his people and continues to speak today
through prophecy, dreams, and vision—always in ways consistent
with the revealed Word of God. Combining biblical study with his
own experience, he shows us not only how to recognize the voice of
God but also how to walk in deeper intimacy and friendship with
the Lord. I highly recommend it!

R. T. Kendall, author of *Prophetic Integrity*

Why I Am Still

SURPRISED

by the

VOICE

of

GOD

Why I Am Still

SURPRISED

by the

VOICE

of

GOD

How God Speaks Today Through
Prophecies, Dreams, and Visions

Updated and Expanded Edition

JACK DEERE

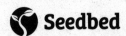

ZONDERVAN REFLECTIVE

Why I Am Still Surprised by the Voice of God
Copyright © 2022 by Jack Deere

Portions of this book were previously published as
Surprised by the Voice of God © 1996

Requests for information should be addressed to:
Zondervan, *3900 Sparks Dr. SE, Grand Rapids, Michigan 49546*

Zondervan titles may be purchased in bulk for educational, business, fundraising, or sales promotional use. For information, please email SpecialMarkets@Zondervan.com.

ISBN 978-0-310-10816-0 (audio)

Library of Congress Cataloging-in-Publication Data

Names: Deere, Jack, author. | Deere, Jack. Why I am surprised by the voice of God.
Title: Why I am still surprised by the voice of God : how God speaks today through
    prophecies, dreams, and visions / Jack Deere.
Description: Updated and expanded edition. | Grand Rapids : Zondervan, 2022. | Portions
    of this book were previously published as Surprised by the voice of God © 1996.
Identifiers: LCCN 2022013415 (print) | LCCN 2022013416 (ebook) | ISBN
    9780310108153 (paperback) | ISBN 9780310113751 (ebook)
Subjects: LCSH: Holy Spirit. | Prophecies. | Dreams—Religious aspects—Christianity. |
    Visions. | Deere, Jack. | BISAC: RELIGION / Christianity / Pentecostal & Charismatic
    | RELIGION / Christian Living / Spiritual Growth
Classification: LCC BT121.3 .D44 2022 (print) | LCC BT121.3 (ebook) | DDC
    234/.13—dc23/eng/20220627
LC record available at https://lccn.loc.gov/2022013415
LC ebook record available at https://lccn.loc.gov/2022013416

Unless otherwise noted, Scripture quotations are taken from The Holy Bible, New International Version®, NIV®. Copyright © 1973, 1978, 1984, 2011 by Biblica, Inc.® Used by permission of Zondervan. All rights reserved worldwide. www.Zondervan.com. The "NIV" and "New International Version" are trademarks registered in the United States Patent and Trademark Office by Biblica, Inc.® • Scripture quotations marked ESV are taken from the ESV® Bible (The Holy Bible, English Standard Version®). Copyright © 2001 by Crossway, a publishing ministry of Good News Publishers. Used by permission. All rights reserved. • Scripture quotations marked KJV are taken from the King James Version. Public domain. • Scripture quotations marked NASB are taken from the (NASB®) New American Standard Bible®, Copyright © 1960, 1971, 1977, 1995 by The Lockman Foundation. Used by permission. All rights reserved. www.lockman.org.

Any internet addresses (websites, blogs, etc.) and telephone numbers in this book are offered as a resource. They are not intended in any way to be or imply an endorsement by Zondervan, nor does Zondervan vouch for the content of these sites and numbers for the life of this book.

All rights reserved. No part of this publication may be reproduced, stored in a retrieval system, or transmitted in any form or by any means—electronic, mechanical, photocopy, recording, or any other—except for brief quotations in printed reviews, without the prior permission of the publisher.

Cover design: Brian Bobel
Cover photo:© YakobchukOlena / iStock photo
Interior design: Kait Lamphere

Printed in the United States of America

22 23 24 25 26 27 28 29 30 31 /TRM/ 14 13 12 11 10 9 8 7 6 5 4 3 2 1

For John Wimber (1934–1997)—
who changed the way the world goes to church.
Churches all over the world now have
ministry teams to pray for those attending services
and worship teams saying "I love you" to God
in beautiful contemporary music.
He was my spiritual father
who taught me and countless others
how to heal and hear the voice of God.

Contents

Chapter 1

The Beginning of a Friendship with God

J esus knew the Bible stone-cold. His enemies discovered this fact the hard way. The young carpenter humiliated the proud professors of the Bible in debate after debate. Yet Jesus claimed that he needed more than his superlative knowledge of the Bible. He had to hear his Father's voice in order to fulfill God's purpose for his life. The only perfect Person, the only one who knew the exact meaning of every single verse of Scripture and how to apply it perfectly, said, "I only speak words my Father gives me, and I only do what I see my Father doing."[1]

The principal enemies of Jesus, the religious elite, had supreme confidence in their knowledge of Scripture, and though some of the elite may have memorized the entire Old Testament, none of them had ever heard the voice of the Father (John 5:37–40).

I, too, was an enemy of Jesus until I heard my first verse of Scripture. I was barely seventeen the night my friend Bruce quoted John 10:28 to me: "I give my sheep eternal life, and they shall never perish; no one will snatch them out

---

1. This is a major theme in the gospel of John (5:19, 30; 7:16; 8:28; 12:49–50; 14:10, 24, 31).

of my hand." That night, I believed in Jesus. I trusted him to forgive my sins and give me new life. On December 18, 1965, at two in the morning, the Light of the world came into my heart. I was no longer a fatherless boy.

Ten years later, I was a professor of the Bible who had never heard the voice of God. I didn't believe in the voice of God. I believed in Scripture. I taught my students not to believe in the voice of God.

After a Hebrew syntax class, one of my students lingered to talk. He said, "The Lord spoke to me and told me to come to seminary."

"The Lord spoke to you?" I asked.

"Yes. Definitely," he replied.

"You mean you heard an audible voice?" I asked.

"No. It was more like an impression," he said.

"An impression?" I asked with incredulity in my tone.

"Is that wrong?" asked the student.

"Are you asking if it's wrong to elevate one of your feelings to the status of the inerrant word of God? I guess it's fine if your goal is to drown in the syrupy seas of existentialism."

This is how I tried to save my students who had fallen into the trap of believing that God still spoke outside of the pages of the Bible. If a student asked about the Lord guiding his followers today, I told him that everything we need for living a godly life is in the Scriptures.

"Well, the Bible doesn't tell me which girl to marry or which church I should pastor," a student objected.

I could twist enough Scripture into my deistic paradigm of spirituality to convince him that the Bible offered an abundance of decision-making principles. He could be 99 percent certain of God's will for his life from Scripture alone.

Some of my colleagues claimed to believe in the "personal leading" of the Lord, but I never heard anyone define that leading or explain how it worked practically. And I never heard a faculty member say, "The Lord led me to . . ." If you had good exegetical skills and common sense, there was no need to stumble into the catacombs of personal leading. And for that tiny area, that 1 percent of life where Scripture was silent, I told students to trust the providence of God, the doctrine that teaches the unseen hand of God guides creation in a way that fulfills all of his purposes. God's purposes are always good, so the students had nothing to worry about.

I did not conclude that God no longer speaks outside of Scripture from a patient and exhaustive study of God's voice in Scripture. My professors taught me the main reason that God did miracles and spoke supernaturally to people in the New Testament was to demonstrate that the apostles were trustworthy teachers of doctrine. The apostles were special people during special times. Now that we had the completed Bible, we were in "normal" times and there was no longer a need for special people or the supernatural voice of God.

When I became a professor of the Bible, a book filled

with miracles and supernatural communications from the Holy Spirit, I believed it was all real and happened just as the authors of the Old and New Testaments had said it happened. But it no longer happened *today*. I claimed that the reason for my unbelief was based on sound exegesis and theology. But that wasn't true. I was afraid of the subjective nature of the voice.

It didn't help that my friends and I had gone to a Pentecostal service when we were in college. It was 1970, and the service was a banner-waving mess. People were coming forward to receive the gift of tongues, so we went down to the front to observe and saw a man on his knees. Another man gripped his right shoulder and yelled, "Just let go, brother." A third man gripped his left shoulder and yelled, "Just hang on, brother." And yet another man stood in front of them all, saying something like, "Shu bosh robo lobo" over and over. The man in front continued, saying, "Just move your mouth. Now let sound come out." Nonsense syllables poured out. "Great," he said, "you've got the gift of tongues. Now help us pray for others." I thought this kind of abuse was normative for anyone who believed in contemporary spiritual gifts. And I wanted nothing to do with it. I had no idea that there was a responsible way to practice spiritual gifts, one that had none of this abuse in it.

When I entered the hard-core world of theological academia, it was drilled into me that feelings were the enemy of rational thought. At the beginning of class, my second-year Greek professor told us, "Liberals feel; we think." We laughed and cheered, glad not to be like those stupid, emotional liberals.[2]

Written statements distilled into theological doctrines could be trusted, but dreams, visions, impressions—how could you even know if they were from God? We had solid hermeneutical principles for interpreting Scripture, but where were the rules for making sense of the ephemeral dramas of our imaginations?

I believed God had gone mute to protect us. And my experience taught me this as well, for outside the Bible, all I heard was divine silence. Surely if God were still speaking to his children like he did in the Bible, he would be speaking like this to me and my colleagues, for we had the soundest theology in the world.

None of the people I trusted ever said God spoke to them. And the people I bumped into who claimed God had spoken to them were not exactly credible.

An older sister of one of my friends showed me her spiral notebooks where she had recorded word for word her *daily* conversations with God. Her confidence that God had revealed amazing truths to her was unshakable, though

---

2. The belief that the moral conflict is the battle between passion and reason is as old as Socrates. The idea that reason is essentially good and passion is intrinsically evil can't be supported by logic or Scripture. See C. S. Lewis's discussion of the rational soul in *The Discarded Image: An Introduction to Medieval and Renaissance Literature* (Cambridge: Cambridge University Press, 1964), 156–60.

some of what she had recorded was nonsense. Most of it was just bland.

Then there was the unhinged guy in my church who said to me that God had told him the Holy Spirit was going to kill his wife because she was disobedient and had ignored all of God's warnings. God also told him he was going to give him a younger, prettier woman in our church to be his new wife. The fact that the prettier woman was married was not a problem, for God had shown him that the Holy Spirit was going to kill her husband because he would not repent of his drug use.

This insanity is exactly what my theology told me would happen if we let a chatty God into our church. The logic was simple. God can only speak inerrant words. Anyone who says God spoke to him is claiming to have heard the inerrant word of God, and therefore he is assuming the same authority as the Scriptures. To believe that God is speaking today like he did in the New Testament is to compromise the authority of Scripture.[3]

---

3. Later I would discover that my "simple logic" contradicted the Scripture. No one who heard the voice of God in the New Testament elevated their experience of hearing the voice to the level of the Scripture's authority. Paul wrote, "If anyone thinks they are a prophet or otherwise gifted by the Spirit, let them acknowledge that what I am writing to you is the Lord's command. But if anyone ignores this, they will themselves be ignored" (1 Corinthians 14:37–38). The Scripture judges all our private communication from God. Even if our private leading is from the Lord, it does not have the same authority as Scripture, which has authority at all times, everywhere, for all believers. The dream that Paul had to go to Macedonia was only for him and his team (Acts 16:9–10). It had no authority over all believers. The fact that it was recorded

I thought the people who believed God had spoken to them personally were emotionally unstable and too lazy to study the Bible, too lazy to learn Greek and Hebrew. My professors had taught me that church history proved only the biblically ignorant believed that miracles or prophetic experiences continued after the Bible was completed. I didn't even know a Pentecostal or charismatic or anyone else who might have been a trustworthy example of someone who had heard God speak outside of Scripture. I lived in the sublime, impenetrable isolation of the biblically elite.

I would have continued to wither in this transcendent superiority, but after a decade of teaching at my seminary, someone I held in high esteem shocked me by telling me he believed in the voice of God, and then he told me credible stories of God speaking to him outside the pages of the Bible. That conversation did not convince me. It provoked me. It launched me into an exhaustive study of the voice of God in Scripture.[4]

Most Christians don't believe what they believe because they made a thorough study of Scripture and came to their conclusions. They believe what they believe because someone they trusted told them what to believe. My professors told me God was no longer speaking outside the pages of

---

in Scripture shows us that one of the ways God will lead us is through dreams. It may also illustrate the importance of doing ministry in teams and making decisions about directions for ministry in teams.

4. I tell the story of this encounter in *Why I Am Still Surprised by the Power of the Spirit* (Grand Rapids: Zondervan, 2020), 17–25.

the Bible, but not one of them had ever made a serious study of the voice of God in Scripture.

In the winter and spring of 1986, I studied every instance of God speaking supernaturally to someone in the New Testament. And in every case, I asked, "Why did you speak to this person? Why was it necessary?"

For the first time, I saw that everyone who had a significant role to play in the New Testament heard the voice of God apart from the Scriptures. They didn't just hear the voice of God; they were dependent on the voice of God to fulfill his highest purposes for their lives.

This was truer of Jesus than anyone else in the New Testament.

It was normal for Jesus to hear from his Father before he did or said things. Jesus said his ministry was guided by this great principle: he only did what he saw his Father doing (John 5:19). John repeatedly emphasized this theme in his gospel. In his humanity, Jesus claims he can do nothing of himself, so he *judges* as he hears his Father judge (5:30). His *teaching* does not originate with himself but with his Father (7:16). He *speaks* only the words of his Father (8:28; 12:49–50; 14:10, 24). In short, he *does* exactly what his Father commands him (14:31). In every instance, Jesus presented himself as a servant under orders in unbroken communion with his Father. And he did these things— judged, taught, spoke, obeyed—not out of his deity but by the Spirit who rested on him without limit (3:34).

To some degree, I had always been aware of Jesus' ability to hear the voice of the Father, but I didn't think it was possible for me to follow his example. Jesus was a special Person. He did miracles and heard the voice of God like no one else. I wasn't special. I also put the apostles in the category of "special." In fact, I put anyone in the New Testament in the category of "special" if they did miracles or heard the voice of God.[5] Without realizing it, I had adopted an anti-supernatural hermeneutic for interpreting the New Testament. Jesus and the apostles were to be our models in everything but the supernatural.

For the first time, I saw how illogical this was. No one ever loved like Jesus loved, but he was still our model of love. Then I saw another flaw in my anti-supernatural hermeneutic. If a perfect person like Jesus needed to hear the voice of his Father, how much more did a flawed person like me need to hear the voice of God? Paul was so sold out to Jesus that he could say, "To me, to live is Christ" (Philippians 1:21). If a person that spiritual needed to hear the voice of God, how much more did someone like me need to hear the voice of God?

I had always assumed the reason they needed the voice of God was that they didn't have the New Testament. But stories like Acts 16:6–10 demolished that assumption.

---

5. It turns out there were a lot of "special" people in the New Testament—so many, in fact, that it is erroneous to argue that the supernatural ministry of the Holy Spirit is only characteristic of a few special people (see appendix 2).

Paul had decided to retrace the steps of his first missionary journey. But along the way, he and Barnabas had such a sharp disagreement over taking Mark with them that they ended their friendship and went separate ways. So Paul chose Silas for his new partner, and off they went. So far, it's just typical Christianity, but after they pick up Timothy in Lystra, the story takes on a new dimension.

> Paul and his companions traveled throughout the region of Phrygia and Galatia, *having been kept by the Holy Spirit from preaching the word in the province of Asia.* When they came to the border of Mysia, they tried to enter Bithynia, *but the Spirit of Jesus would not allow them to.* So they passed by Mysia and went down to Troas. *During the night Paul had a vision* of a man of Macedonia standing and begging him, "Come over to Macedonia and help us." After Paul had seen the vision, we got ready at once to leave for Macedonia, concluding that God had called us to preach the gospel to them.
>
> *Acts 16:6–10, my emphasis*[6]

What a strange story! On all the missionary trips I've been on, we preached the gospel everywhere we traveled. But the Holy Spirit forbade Paul, Silas, and Timothy from

---

6. Paul was actually being led to a group of women in Philippi initially and not to "a man," as depicted in the vision. This teaches us not to assume that all visions will be literally fulfilled.

preaching the gospel on the first part of their journey. The Scripture does not tell us how the Holy Spirit kept Paul and his team from preaching the gospel in Asia. Whether it was through a hindering circumstance or through a direct communication, the point is that Paul knew how to recognize the voice of God in his head and in his circumstances.[7] The second point is that God had a plan for this missionary journey, and he had only just begun to unfold that plan. With Asia off-limits, they headed north and attempted to turn east to preach the gospel in Bithynia, but the Spirit of Jesus said no. They had been forbidden by God to preach in the south, in the north and in the east, so they headed west down to Troas. And Paul received the night vision.[8]

This is not the kind of guidance someone could ever get from reading the Bible. God cared where Paul preached the gospel. To fulfill God's highest purposes for his life, Paul had to be able to hear God's voice outside the Bible.

When Paul set out on his second missionary journey, he had no idea that God would lead him to carry the gospel

---

7. Paul wrote to the Thessalonians, "For we wanted to come to you—certainly I, Paul, did, again and again—but Satan blocked our way" (1 Thessalonians 2:18). Paul could tell the difference between Satan hindering and the Holy Spirit forbidding. This makes a huge practical difference. We can fight against Satan's hindering, but we must submit to God's forbidding.

8. This story shows that even when the night vision or dream is definitely from the Lord, it may not be given with absolute certainty regarding its authenticity or its meaning. The group "concluded" after a discussion that the dream was from God, and it meant they were supposed to go to Macedonia. They couldn't come to a conclusion without first having a discussion about the nature and meaning of the dream.

from Asia into Europe. A group of women had been meeting by a river on the Sabbath to pray. God heard their prayers and dragged his eminent apostle across a continent and deposited him at that riverbank. Then he opened Lydia's heart to believe, and the church at Philippi was born. God used Paul's decision to retrace the steps of his first missionary journey, two negative commands by the Holy Spirit, a night vision, and the prayers of a group of women to bring his life and power to the city of Philippi.

These kinds of stories opened my eyes to see how God built the church in Acts: dedication to Jesus, prayer, *and* the Holy Spirit's supernatural guidance and miraculous power.

I told one of my smartest colleagues and best friends at the seminary that Acts 16:6–10 proved that God did speak to us outside of the Scriptures. "You can't use that passage," he said. "That was the apostle Paul, not an ordinary Christian. And besides, the book of Acts took place at the crossroads of salvation history. They had to get the foundation right back then." But it made no sense to argue that God cared where Paul planted churches but didn't care where we plant churches, or that he wanted to get the foundation right but didn't care how we built on it.

After being jolted awake by Acts 16:6–10, I crashed into 1 Corinthians 14:1:

> *Follow the way of love and eagerly desire gifts of the Spirit, especially prophecy.*

I had read and memorized the Bible religiously for over twenty years and never given this verse a moment's reflection. In the spring of 1986, I stared at that verse and thought, *This text can't mean what it seems to say.* I couldn't think of a better way to create a chaotic church than to command the church members to prophesy. What good could come from church members running around saying to each other, "God told me to tell you . . ."?

It was tempting to say that by the gift of prophecy Paul meant "inspired teaching" or "passionate preaching." But I was a professor of exegesis and a lexicographer, a specialist in defining Greek and Semitic words, so that kind of sloppy, dishonest way of explaining away Scripture was not open to me. I looked up every single use of *prophecy* and *prophesy* in the New Testament. In 1 Corinthians, Paul demonstrated it was impossible to define what he meant by prophecy as inspired teaching, for according to him the gift of teaching and the gift of prophecy were two distinct gifts (12:28–31).

The gift of prophecy in the New Testament is supernatural revelation given by the Holy Spirit for at least four purposes. First, prophets predicted the future to help believers prepare for the future (Acts 11:28–30). Second, prophets revealed the present priorities of God for individuals or groups (13:1–3). Third, prophets used the Holy Spirit's revelation to encourage and strengthen believers (15:32; 27:21–26). And fourth, the gift of prophecy that Paul had in mind could also be used in the worship service to reveal

15

the secrets in the hearts of unbelievers attending so that they fell on their faces and declared that God was really present in the meeting (1 Corinthians 14:24–25). Paul knew a true prophetic gift has more power over the hearts of unbelievers than our best intellectual arguments.

Next to the gift of helps, prophecy is probably the most widely distributed gift in the body of Christ. On the day of Pentecost, the church was born in the fire of prophecy. Peter used Joel 2:28–32 to define what the Holy Spirit was doing on that day:

> "In the last days, God says,
>
> > I will pour out my Spirit on all[9] people.
>
> Your sons and daughters will prophesy,
>
> > your young men will see visions,
> >
> > your old men will dream dreams.
>
> Even on my servants, both men and women,
>
> > I will pour out my Spirit in those days,
> >
> > and they will prophesy.
>
> I will show wonders in the heavens above
>
> > and signs on the earth below,
> >
> > blood and fire and billows of smoke.

---

9. In Greek, the word *all* is used like the English word. It can mean "all without exception" (the totality of). It can mean "the majority of." Or it can mean "all kinds of." The context of Acts 2:17–21 shows that it means "all kinds of." The Holy Spirit will be poured out on all kinds of people without regard for gender or age.

The sun will be turned to darkness
and the moon to blood
before the coming of the great and glorious
day of the Lord.

And everyone who calls
on the name of the Lord will be saved."[10]

Acts 2:17–21

In the Old Testament, prophetic ministry belonged to the men.[11] But when the Holy Spirit moved into his new temple, the human heart, he no longer observed gender or age distinctions. He enabled men, women, and children to prophesy. The preeminent, defining spiritual gift of the church, the gift we are all commanded to emphasize in the

---

10. Another thing important to understand about Joel's prophecy is that it has a near and far fulfillment, a common feature of several biblical prophecies. Joel 2:28–29 (Acts 2:17–18) was fulfilled on the day of Pentecost when the Holy Spirit took up residence in the hearts of believers. The "wonders" of Joel 2:30–31 (Acts 2:19–20) will take place just before Jesus returns to consummate his kingdom. The purpose of the miraculous ministry of the Spirit, whether at the beginning of the church or at the return of Jesus, is to move people to call on the name of the Lord that they may be brought into the eternal family of God (Joel 2:32; Acts 2:21).

11. In the Old Testament, there is one prominent example of a prophetic child, Samuel (1 Samuel 3:1–21), and three named prophetesses (Miriam in Exodus 15:20; Deborah in Judges 4:4; and Huldah in 2 Kings 22:14). Isaiah's wife is not named (Isaiah 8:3), and Noadiah is usually considered a false prophetess (Nehemiah 6:14, along with the false prophetesses of Ezekiel 13:17). Another way to view the gender disparity is that *prophet* is used 306 times in the Hebrew Bible, while *prophetess* is used six times.

church, is not teaching but prophecy.[12] The primary purpose of the gift of prophecy is to move the hearts of believers and unbelievers to call on the name of the Lord. Perhaps more than any other church in history, the church in Acts called on the name of the Lord and grew at enormous rates. Every chapter in the book of Acts has an example or a report of the miraculous ministry of the Holy Spirit, with prophecy and hearing the voice of God being the dominating categories of this supernatural ministry.[13]

After months of pondering all the New Testament passages that taught about the voice of God and prophesying, I was convinced that I should expect God to speak to me outside the Scriptures, but I didn't have a clue how to hear his voice. I had no credible witness in my spiritual circles to teach me, and the fear of drowning in those syrupy seas of existentialism danced through my nightmares. It was hard to shake the feeling that my feelings were enemies to be defeated, not something God could use to reveal truth about me and to me. But by some mystery of his love, I had been given the gift of a teachable heart, and God sent gifted people to help me hear the voice of love.

When I first came to believe in the voice, I thought hearing the voice of God was mainly about receiving his

---

12. Not every Christian has the spiritual gift of prophecy (1 Corinthians 12:29), but the church service that Paul envisioned had two or three prophets speaking in every service.

13. See appendix 1 for a listing of these examples.

guidance for our ministries. I didn't know that Jesus wanted more than my service. He wanted a friend, and friends talk with each other. This book is the story of how I learned to hear the voice of Jesus and how I became his friend—not a great friend, but a friend—someone who frequently feels Jesus' love and enjoys being with him.

Chapter 2

Awakened to the Ministry
of the Holy Spirit

Though he has been gone for a quarter of a century and most Christians today have never heard of him, when I knew him, he was the most loved *and* most hated pastor of the twentieth century. His enemies claimed that the devil had raised him up to lead Christians away from the Bible. I thought God had raised him up to lead us back to the kind of church described in the Bible. When I met him, I was still a tenured associate professor of Hebrew exegesis and Semitic languages, who could also teach New Testament Greek at the graduate level. But this professor couldn't hear the voice of God, and I had never seen a supernatural healing.

My wife, Leesa, and I met John Wimber in the spring of 1986 while he was doing a conference at a Southern Baptist church in my city, Fort Worth, Texas. We became instant friends. John did huge conferences all over the world on healing, hearing the voice of God, and the gifts of the Spirit. John taught people sane ways to use the spiritual gifts to build up the church rather than blow it up. The conferences began by worshiping God with beautiful contemporary music. Then John or a team member gave a practical message on some aspect of supernatural ministry. The message was followed by a ministry time in which John or another speaker would "see" or "hear" by revelation conditions or people God wanted to heal. John didn't just talk about supernatural ministry; he demonstrated it without any hype or hoopla.

John paid my and Leesa's way to any conference we could attend.

At one of the first conferences I went to in 1986, about seven hundred people were in attendance. Near the beginning of the ministry time, John said, "There is a man here who was in a shower and inhaled something, and it's made you sick. Please come forward so we can pray for you." I thought, *That's weird. I don't think that's true.* Then a man came forward. He had been doing some work on a shower, knocked over a chemical, and inhaled it, and his raw throat wouldn't heal.

After the meeting, I asked, "John, how did you know about the man in the shower?"

"I saw it happening," he said. "Sometimes I look at someone in the audience and 'know' what their illness is, but often I will 'see' pictures or little film clips of what is wrong or how they were injured. Sometimes when I see a picture, the Lord will interpret it for me."

That night when we tried to walk out of the building, people kept stopping John and asking him for prayer. He prayed for each one. He often knew facts about their lives without people telling him. At the back of the room, a man was slumped over in a chair and shaking. His wife clung to him and wept over him. People were praying for him. John stopped, looked at the couple's name tags, and said to the wife, "June, let go of your husband for just a minute. He's going to be all right." Then he leaned down and whispered something in the husband's ear that no one else could hear. The man nodded his head in agreement. Then John placed his hand on the husband's head and said, "I break the power of the enemy's plan for this couple in the name of Jesus." The shaking stopped.

When we were out of earshot, I asked, "What was that all about?" John had seen the man's sexual bondage. When John whispered it in his ear, the man nodded yes, confessing the sin that John had seen.

I had been with John when God healed the blind and the deaf, straightened crooked bones, and did other miracles. In just a year and half, I had seen a lot of healing in the Vineyard, but no prophecy. I had seen a lot of supernatural revelation preceding the healings. Frequently, a Vineyard speaker would point to a section of the crowd and say, "There is a young man in this section, and you have lumbar pain and feel heat in your back right now. Come up to the front and let us pray for you." It was all true, and the young man was healed. We didn't call that kind of revelation "prophecy." We called it "a word of knowledge." (Technically, no one but Paul and the Holy

Spirit know what a "word of knowledge" is, since Paul used the expression only once in 1 Corinthians 12:8, but never defined it.)

Then I heard about the "Kansas City Prophets," who were alleged to be heart-stopping prophets. A friend who knew these prophets offered to introduce them to me. I called John and told him I was going to meet the KC prophets. "Jack," he said, "I know those guys. I've seen them minister. They're not impressive. We've got better prophets here in the Vineyard. God gave you a good mind. If you go up there, use it. Don't get deceived." My desire to meet prophets turned into determination not to be deceived.

In the fall of 1987, I went to Kansas City and met the pastor of prophets, Mike Bickle. Five years younger than me, he was built like a short fullback who could bench three hundred pounds and run over linebackers with ease. He had an infectious joy and made you feel like the most important person in the room. He arranged a meeting with one of the prophets.

The next morning at 8:00 a.m., Leesa and I went to a room in the basement of the church with five of our friends from Fort Worth. I was the last one to enter, and I could hear Mike's deep, resonant voice booming from inside. A scary-looking guy stood just inside the door. He was built like a tight end, a little under six feet tall with a salt-and-pepper beard and a head of hair to match, and he looked like he'd been dressed by Eddie Bauer himself. It was the deep-set eyes in combination with the beard that made him look spooky. He looked surprised when he saw me. He said, "I didn't expect to see you here this morning." Already, I didn't like this cocky show-off. "What do you mean?" I said. "I don't even know you."

"Well, I know you. Eight nights ago, I had a dream about you. I thought it was important so I wrote it down. Would you like to hear what the Lord showed me about you?"

"Yes," is what I said. But what I thought was, *Take your best shot. I'm not going to be deceived by you.*

I followed him into the room. Everyone was already seated in a circle of orange plastic chairs that clashed with the bright green carpet. I thought, *Well, they sure don't waste any money on decorators around here.*

I sat down beside Leesa. The Eddie Bauer boy sat opposite me. I stared at him and turned my face to granite. If he tried to cold read me, I would savor the frustration on his face. God gave me a mind, and this preppy prophet boy was not going to get inside it.

His name was John Paul Jackson.

"You have a prayer," he said in his soft, soothing, Southern accent. I liked his gentle voice. "It's really more than a prayer. It is one of the major dreams of your heart." Then he told me the prayer I had prayed that morning, the prayer I prayed every morning, because it was the dream of my heart.

Then he said, "God said to tell you that this dream is from him, and he's going to give you what you're asking for."

My heart exploded with joy. It took all my self-control not to burst into tears because God is so wonderful to me. But I regrouped on the inside and stared right back into his eyes like the words meant nothing to me.

My dream, both then and now, is grandiose. I have always kept it to myself, because I've learned over the years that sometimes we can lose our dreams if we reveal them before they come to pass. I've seen people lose what were probably true prophetic promises by revealing them ahead of time to increase their stature in the eyes of others.

Then he said, "You had a father who dropped the ball on you."

When I was twelve years old, the oldest of four children, my thirty-nine-year-old father—the hero I worshiped— committed suicide with his childhood rifle on our living room couch. He left a pretty, thirty-four-year-old widow with a tenth-grade education to care for his four children. We fell into poverty, alcoholism, and sexual immorality. I had dreams of Dad burning in the fiery caverns of hell. When I thought about Dad, a demonic voice in my head said, *You will kill yourself before you turn forty, just like your dad did.* I told no one about that voice. It spoke to me regularly, even after I was born again. It left the night I turned forty.

So, yes, my father did drop the ball on me.

"The Lord is going to make up for the loss of your father. He will send you new fathers. You won't just learn from one man. You will have the father you need for each new stage in your life."

He misinterpreted the revelation that God had sent him. He saw my past as the future. What he prophesied was exactly what God *had* done for me. As soon as I became a believer at seventeen, God began to send me fathers. I joined a Southern Baptist church two weeks after I became a Christian. Men in the church bragged on me and brought me into their stable homes to eat at their family tables and watch football games. I saw husbands kiss their wives in public, and I wanted a family like theirs.

Three months into my new life, God sent me a great Young Life leader to disciple me for the next five years. His name was Scott Manley. He was twenty-seven and a recent graduate of the Baptist seminary. He was everything I wanted to be—handsome, athletic, intelligent, a great speaker, funny, and so confident. He loved me and taught me to love what Jesus loved. He was my best friend, big brother, and spiritual father for the next five years. I became a Young Life leader like him and led many high school kids to Christ and then discipled them like Scott had done for me.

When I went to Dallas Seminary, the three greatest scholars of the seminary—two Greek professors and one

Hebrew professor—became my academic fathers and gave me priceless skills in the biblical languages, in interpreting Scripture, and in theology—skills I don't think I could have acquired anywhere else. Their offices were always open to me, and they praised me privately and publicly.

And now I had John Wimber teaching me the supernatural ministry of the Holy Spirit. God had made up for the loss of my father by giving me a series of exceptional spiritual fathers.

His prophecy was true. He simply got the timing wrong. And timing is one of the most difficult things to get right in a prophetic revelation. Prophets who accurately predicted the coming of the Messiah searched their writings, "trying to find out the time and circumstances to which the Spirit of Christ in them was pointing when he predicted the sufferings of the Messiah and the glories that would follow" (1 Peter 1:11).

However, until that moment, I had never seen how the wisdom of God used the loss of my father to turn me into the man I had become. He gave me great fathers at each new stage of my life to do for me what Dad could never have done. The wisdom of God is amazing. Nothing can spoil his plan. I was worshiping God on the inside. I am worshiping him now as I write these words. God has been a great Father to me.

All John Paul saw was my unflinching stare.

"When you were young, the Lord gave you athletic

30

ability, but he allowed you to be frustrated in the use of it. This was so you would put all your effort into cultivating your intellect. You've done that. You're sitting on top of an intellectual kingdom now, but it hasn't brought you what you expected, and you are heartsick."

John Paul had just called out the greatest frustration and pain of my teen years. I had told no one about it, not even Leesa. Whether it was an injury or my chaotic family life, something beyond my control always kept me from glory on the baseball diamond or the football field while my best friends wore the varsity jackets.

Then I became a believer, and it turned out that God had given me a mind that could memorize huge quantities of Scripture and understand the writings of C. S. Lewis. When I came to Dallas Seminary in 1971, my first-year theology professor handed me the bibliography for the course. I had already read every book on it.

When I turned seventeen, I did not know a single verse of Scripture. When I turned twenty-seven, I had become a professor of Old Testament exegesis and Semitic languages at Dallas Seminary. I taught the most difficult courses in the seminary. I could do lexicographic work in multiple languages and offer decent criticisms of liberal Old Testament scholarship. Being called Professor Deere was better than batting cleanup—at first.

Gradually, the intoxication wore off. As I entered my twelfth year of teaching, I knew that most students would never look at a Hebrew lexicon once they graduated. No one in their church would ever ask them if Moses wrote the Pentateuch or if it was produced by some anonymous scribal school in the sixth century BC. What I was teaching was irrelevant to the students' lives and ministries.

Christians on the outside seemed to think that being on the faculty of a seminary was like being in the holy of holies. It's not. The same pettiness, inconsistency, backbiting, lying, hypocrisy, divorce, adultery, and other sins that are found in any church also festered in our faculty. It had to. No one stops sinning until they go to heaven. I sinned my share of sins while I was on the faculty. Our worst sin was our blatant spiritual pride. We told our students that our seminary was the best seminary in the world and that our doctrine was the best in the world. I believed as a student and as a faculty member that we were the most skilled interpreters and teachers of the Bible. Feeling superior to just about everyone had withered my heart.[1]

---

1. My seminary was not unique in claiming that it was the best seminary in the world. I talk with graduates from other evangelical seminaries and from denominational seminaries who say their professors claimed the same superiority. Paul warned us a long time ago that love edifies, but knowledge puffs up (1 Corinthians 8:1). No one goes to seminary to learn to love; they go to get smart.

By the time I sat there opposite John Paul, seminary had become nothing more than my day job. If I weren't sick at heart over my day job, I was surely cynical of heart.

"All this frustration was meant by God to prepare you for the call that God has on your life," said the soothing Southern voice that I was beginning to love.

Next subject.

"You are in a conflict now, and you think there are only three people on your side. The Lord says to tell you there are five more on your side."

John Paul was amazing. I *was* in a conflict, and I thought there were only three people on my side. No one except Leesa knew about this conflict.

Then he told me about my future, the place and purpose where all this frustration and pain were meant to lead. Because he was so accurate about my past and present, I believed what he said about my future. Some of it has come true, but the greater part that is related to my grandiose dream has yet to come true. I'm still praying for the prophecy rather than publishing it.

John Paul missed the timing on the part about my spiritual fathers. So, some would argue that it wasn't a perfect word. But who of us preachers have ever preached a perfect sermon? Even if it wasn't a perfect word, it was a priceless word to me. It caused me to love and worship God more.

John Paul said, "Well, that's all I have for you."

"Thank you," I said without an ounce of feeling in my voice or expression on my face.

"You're welcome," he said.

Then he prophesied over Leesa. She wept after the first minute.

Mike Bickle and I were the last ones to leave the room. As we climbed the stairs, he asked, "Was anything that John Paul said over you true?"

"Every bit of it. It was amazing," I said.

"But your face said none of it was true. The whole time John Paul was prophesying over you, I thought, *I've never seen John Paul miss it so badly.*"

"Wimber warned me not to be deceived," I said.

"Oh, now I understand," said Mike.

I never recovered from that first meeting with John Paul on that September Saturday in 1987. I had never felt the love, the power, and the wonder of God all at once like I did that morning. I was ruined. In the space of twenty minutes, the prophetic Spirit of Christ had rewired me. I felt like the Samaritan woman at the well.[2] I wanted to shout to all my friends, "Come, see a prophet who told me everything I ever did." I knew I could never again be happy without the Holy Spirit's prophetic ministry.

---

2. John 4.

John Paul's word has helped me to survive some beatings and has kept my dream alive ever since. It still strengthens me and gives me hope by the Holy Spirit. And more than thirty years later, it still makes me say, "I love you, God. You are amazing."

I told John Wimber about John Paul's ministry over us. He was impressed and eventually came to love John Paul.[3]

---

3. John Wimber's original negative opinion of the Kansas City Prophets was based on his initial meeting of Bob Jones years earlier without seeing him prophesy. Bob was raised in immorality and ignorance in the backwoods of Arkansas. He dropped out of school in the third grade. He was incapable of producing a single sentence without a grammatical error. He was saved in an insane asylum when he was thirty-nine. The audible voice of God interrupted his plan to commit suicide in the asylum. He was one of the most amazing prophets I have ever seen. Wimber came to love Bob and brought him and John Paul to Anaheim to prophesy over all the church staff. My experience with Bob taught me never to judge "the package" in which the prophets come.

Chapter 3

The Miracles of the
Scottish Covenanters

In my second meeting with John Wimber in May 1986, he told me that if I became his friend, my seminary would fire me, but I didn't believe him. A tenured professor can't be fired. One year after I met him, my seminary fired me for becoming his friend. My last day at seminary was December 18, 1987, exactly twenty-two years after I gave my heart to Jesus in the middle of the night. My seminary would not give me a chance to defend what I believed. It hurt my pride, but John Paul had given me hope that God had something better for me.

In the fall of 1988, the year after I was fired, my radio-active friend brought me on staff at his church in Anaheim, California, where thousands of people worshiped Jesus every Sunday and where people came from all over the world to see a modern church that sometimes looked a little like the church in the book of Acts.

A year or so later, John brought John Paul on our staff to be the prophetic trainer.

One Sunday evening, instead of going to our adult service, I grabbed John Paul and said, "Hey, let's spend the evening with our ten- to twelve-year-old kids." There were about two hundred of these kids in a room in the back of the huge warehouse where our church met. When we got them all seated on the floor, I told them they could ask me any question they wanted. It could be about the Bible, the church, what it was like to be a pastor, or anything else they wanted to ask. I hadn't even thought to pray about the evening. I was confident the kids would be impressed with my knowledge of the Bible.

The first kid raised his hand. "Pastor Jack," he said, "why is it that bad things happen to people who love God and try to follow him?"

Hmm, I thought, *why* do *bad things happen to good people?* Theologians have grappled with the problem of suffering for two thousand years, and it is still the major argument against the existence of a good and omnipotent God. I mumbled some sort of answer about God not wanting robots but rather friends with the freedom and dignity of true choice.

A second hand went up. "Pastor Jack, why did God create the devil?"

Hmm, I thought, *why* did *God create the devil?* Again, I mumbled some sort of answer about God not wanting robots but rather friends with freedom and dignity. Now, I was boring the kids. It went on like this for forty-five minutes. Some demon from hell had smuggled in a list of all the unsolved theological problems from the last twenty centuries and said, "Here, kids, ask him these." I retired from the business of answering theological questions and said to John Paul, "Has the Lord shown you anything about these kids? He hasn't shown me a thing."

"Yes," he said. "He has spoken to me about this young lady," pointing to a skinny, freckle-faced, twelve-year-old girl with long red hair sitting in the front row, "about that young man back there," pointing to a twelve-year-old boy sitting in the middle of the room, "and about this lady," pointing to one of the Sunday school teachers at the back of the room.

"What's your name?" he asked the girl in the front row.

"J-J-Julie." Julie was not sure she wanted the bearded man with spooky eyes to give her a prophetic word in front of two hundred of her peers.

"Julie, while Pastor Jack was talking, I had a vision of you. It was Tuesday night. You went to your bedroom and shut the door. You were crying. You looked up to heaven and said, 'God, do you love me? I have to know—do you really love me?' God didn't say anything to you on Tuesday night, but he sent me here tonight to tell you that he loves you. *He really loves you, Julie.* He also told me to tell you that the trouble going on around you is not your fault. He didn't tell me what he is going to do about the trouble, but he wants you to know that you aren't the cause of it."

Then he went on to say something to the twelve-year-old boy and to the Sunday school teacher. After he had finished, I called those three people up to the front to talk privately. I wanted to make sure everything John Paul had said was true and to give them a chance to ask any questions they may have had.

"Julie, last Tuesday night, were you in your bedroom crying, and did you ask God if he really loved you?" I asked.

"Yes," she said.

"Are your parents fighting now?"

"Yes."

"Are they talking about getting a divorce?"

"Yes."

"Do you think that's your fault?"

She looked up at me, smiled, and said, "Not anymore."

I walked out of church that night thinking about a twelve-year-old boy who could not separate his sins from his parents' sins. My father "divorced" my mother by committing suicide when I was twelve years old. I know what it's like to grow up angry and hopeless, feeling like a mistake.

Then I thought about a twelve-year-old girl in Anaheim who maybe, just maybe, wouldn't be sitting in a psychiatrist's office when she was thirty years old, trying to get rid of undeserved guilt she had carried around for the last twenty years. And I thought about two hundred other kids who saw that the God they talk about in church is real and knows everything about their lives and loves them in spite of it.

I stood before the kids that night with a Bible in my hand and a decent knowledge of its contents. But my Bible didn't tell me that the redheaded twelve-year-old girl on the front row was dying under false guilt. And she would have never told anyone about the trouble in her home. I never breathed a word to anyone about the sickness in my home when I was a kid. Sick homes guard their secrets. The only way she could have gotten any help was through the prophetic word. That is one reason why the apostle Paul told us to pursue the gift of prophecy more than any other spiritual gift. Perhaps no other spiritual gift brings hope and the love of God into a person's life like the gift of prophecy.

This kind of supernatural ministry happened regularly in John Wimber's church, the Vineyard Christian Fellowship of Anaheim, California. And though some seminary professors claimed otherwise, there has never been a period in history since Jesus introduced the ministry of the Holy Spirit to his church where the Holy Spirit has not been doing these kinds of things.

Miracles and Prophecies among the Scottish Reformers

When I first started searching historical records for miracles, I skipped the Reformation because the Reformers taught that miracles had ceased and that God only spoke through Scripture. Martin Luther (1483–1546) led the Reformation in Germany. John Calvin (1509–1564) fled to

Switzerland from France and is considered by many to be the preeminent theologian of the Reformation. When I was in seminary, I read widely in Luther and Calvin and also in the English Reformers, many of whom became martyrs. I never studied the history of the Reformation in Scotland. I only dabbled a little bit in the theology of John Knox, but beyond his feud with Mary, Queen of Scots, I knew nothing of his personal life.

A few years after I left my seminary, I spent several days in the basement of the library at the University of Edinburgh in Scotland with some of their theological graduates, searching the original historical records of the Scottish Reformation. I was amazed to find out that for almost two hundred years in Scotland, miracles were happening, things like raising the dead and healing the insane and epileptics, and staggering prophecies were fulfilled among a people who had a rock-solid theology and who were willing to die for Jesus and who did die for Jesus. Here is a brief account of the ministries of some of the leaders of the Scottish Reformation.

George Wishart (ca. 1513–1546)

George Wishart was one of the early Scottish Reformers and a mentor of John Knox who claimed that Wishart "was so clearly illuminated with the spirit of prophecy, that he saw not only things pertaining to himself, but also such things as some towns, and the whole realm afterwards felt, which he forespake, not in secret, but in the audience of many."[1]

David Beaton, cardinal and archbishop of St Andrews, hated Wishart because the people held him in high esteem and because he viewed him as a threat to international political alliances he valued.[2]

Wishart's public lectures on the book of Romans were so well attended in Dundee that Beaton had the local magistrate publicly forbid Wishart to preach again in that city.[3] After the magistrate, Robert Mill, delivered the charge, Wishart looked toward heaven and remained silent for a while. No one moved. Then at last he said,

> God is my witness that I never minded your trouble,
> but your comfort . . . but sure I am, to reject the Word
> of God, and drive away His messengers, is not the way
> to save you from trouble, but to bring you into it. When
> I am gone . . . if it be long well with, I am not led by the

---

1. John Knox, *History of the Reformation*, vol. 1, ed. William Croft Dickinson (New York: Philosophical Library, 1950), 60.

2. See Nigel M. de S. Cameron, ed., *Dictionary of Scottish Church History and Theology* (Edinburgh: T&T Clark, 1993), 65–66.

3. *The Scots Worthies* by John Howie (ed. W. H. Carslaw [1775; repr., Edinburgh: Oliphant, Anderson, & Ferrier, 1902]) contains a short biography of Wishart (18–32), as well as Knox's *History* (48–66), from which the account above is drawn. In several quotations throughout this chapter, I have removed the Scotticisms and modernized the spelling and grammar.

Spirit of Truth; and if unexpected trouble come upon you, remember this is the cause, and turn to God by repentance, for He is merciful.[4]

Wishart left Dundee and went elsewhere to preach.

Four days later, a severe plague broke out in Dundee. A month later, news of the plague reached Wishart, who was then in western Scotland. He returned immediately to Dundee and comforted the sufferers. When he arrived, he stood at the east gate and preached a sermon on Psalm 107:20: "He sent out his word and healed them; he rescued them from the grave." Wishart risked his life caring for the infected people until the plague abated.

Through supernatural revelation, Wishart escaped two public attempts on his life. He prophesied in 1545 that the town of Haddington would be judged with a severe plague followed by bondage to foreigners. This was fulfilled in 1548–49, when the town was destroyed by the English. The plague was so severe it hindered the burial of the dead.

Wishart escaped Cardinal Beaton's first attempt on his life, but he predicted the cardinal would ultimately kill him. When Wishart was with Knox at Haddington, God revealed to Wishart that his death was near. As Wishart was leaving Haddington, Knox begged him to let him go along

---

4. Howie, *Scots Worthies*, 20.

with him to Ormiston. Wishart declined, saying, "One is sufficient for one sacrifice." At Ormiston, Cardinal Beaton had Wishart arrested, and through a series of political intrigues and an illegal trial, he had him condemned to be burned at the stake for heresy.

On March 1, 1546, the executioners came to Wishart's cell, put a rope around his neck, tied his hands behind his back, and fastened sacks of gunpowder on his body. The gunpowder was meant to hasten his death and spare him some of the pain of being burned to death. The guards led him to a specially built scaffold just opposite the fore tower of the cardinal's palace in St Andrews. Rich cushions had been placed in the windows of the tower so the cardinal and his guests could watch the spectacle in comfort. When the executioner tied Wishart to the stake, he prayed for his accusers, asking God to forgive them. The executioner was so moved by this that he asked Wishart's forgiveness. To which Wishart replied, "Come hither." When his executioner drew near, Wishart kissed his cheek and said, "I forgive you. Do your work." The man turned and lit the fire. The gunpowder blew up, but Wishart was still alive. When the captain of the castle guard saw this, he told the dying man to be of good courage. Wishart replied, "This flame has scorched my body; yet it has not daunted my spirit." Then, referring to Cardinal Beaton, he continued. "He who, from yonder place, looks upon me with such pride, shall, within a few days, lie in the same [i.e., the same castle], as ignominiously as he is now seen proudly to rest himself." These were the last words of George Wishart. He was the Stephen of the Scottish Reformed Church and a forerunner of revival and renewal.

On May 28, 1546, less than three months after Wishart's death, at fifty-two years of age, Cardinal David Beaton was murdered in his palace, and his body was hung out of the window from which he had watched Wishart's martyrdom, fulfilling Wishart's last prophecy.

John Knox (ca. 1514–1572)

Many of the people of Scotland also believed John Knox to be a prophet. No less an authority than James Melville, divinity professor at the University of St Andrews, referred to him as the "Paul and apostle of our nation."[5] One of Knox's most famous prophecies is quoted by several of his biographers. While on his deathbed, Knox asked his friends David Lindsay and James Lawson to go to the Lord of Grange, William Kirkaldy, whom Knox loved. Kirkaldy was attempting to hold the castle of Edinburgh

---

5. Quoted in Jasper Ridley, *John Knox* (Oxford: Clarendon, 1968), 504. Ridley wrote, "The stories about Knox's prophetic powers, showing how his prophecies came true, were also circulated within a very few years of his death by Smeton, and were later repeated and elaborated by James Melville and many other Scottish Protestant writers" (526).

for Mary, Queen of Scots, against the English army. Knox said:

> Go, I pray you, and tell him from me, in the name of God, that unless he leave that evil course wherein he has entered, neither shall that rock [the castle of Edinburgh] . . . afford him any help, nor the carnal wisdom of that man, whom he counteth half a god [William Maitland of Lethington, Mary's former secretary of state]; but he shall be pulled out of that nest, and brought down over the wall with shame, and his carcass shall be hung before the sun; so God hath assured me.[6]

Lindsay and Lawson delivered the message, but Kirkaldy ignored Knox's warning. On May 29, 1573, Kirkaldy was forced to surrender the castle. The castle gate was blocked with fallen stones due to the English bombardment. Just as Knox had prophesied, Kirkaldy was lowered over the wall by a rope in shame. On August 3, 1573, Kirkaldy was hanged at the Mercat Cross of Edinburgh. He was facing east, away from the sun, but before he died, his body swung around to the west, so that he was "hung before the sun," just as Knox had prophesied.[7]

---

6. Quoted in Howie, *Scots Worthies*, 60; see also Ridley, *John Knox*, 517, 519.
7. Ridley, *John Knox*, 519.

John Welsh (ca. 1570–1622)

John Welsh was another of the Scottish Reformers who showed remarkable prophetic powers. Samuel Rutherford (1600–1661), one of the most famous of the Scottish Reformed theologians, called Welsh "that heavenly prophetical and apostolic man of God."[8] After spending some of his early years as a prodigal, Welsh returned to the Lord and married John Knox's daughter Elizabeth.

By all accounts, Welsh was an extraordinarily godly man. It was said of him that "he reckoned the day ill-spent if he stayed not seven or eight hours in prayer."[9] When he became the pastor of the church of Ayr, it was not uncommon for him to spend the whole night in prayer at the church.[10]

Many of Welsh's prophecies have been recorded, along with their fulfillment. He prophesied accurately about various individuals' prosperity, blessing, and vocation. For example, while Welsh was the pastor at Kirkcudbright, he told a wealthy young man, Robert Glendinning, that he ought to start studying the Scriptures because he would succeed Welsh in the pastoral ministry at Kirkcudbright. The man gave no indication at all that he had any interest

---

8. Quoted in Robert Fleming, *The Fulfilling of the Scripture* (1669; repr., Rotterdam: n.p., 1671), 424.

9. Howie, *Scots Worthies*, 120.

10. See Howie, *Scots Worthies*, 122.

in a pastoral career, nor was there any other evidence to lead Welsh to this conclusion, yet it came to pass.[11]

Welsh was also famous for prophesying judgments over individuals. On several occasions, he prophesied the loss of house and property to individuals who refused to repent. These judgments came true.[12] He was also known to have prophesied the unexpected deaths of a number of individuals, the most dramatic of which came while Welsh was being held prisoner in Edinburgh Castle before he was sent into exile.

One night at supper, he was speaking of the Lord and his Word to all who were sitting at the table. Everyone at the table was edified by Welsh's conversation, with the exception of one young man who laughed and sometimes mocked him. Welsh endured this for a while but then abruptly stopped in the middle of his discourse. Welsh's face turned sad, and he told everyone at the dinner table to be silent "and observe the work of the Lord upon that mocker." Immediately, the young man sank beneath the table and died.[13]

During the time the great plague was raging all over Scotland, the city of Ayr had been spared. The city magistrates set guards at each of the entrances of the city to protect it from being infected by any suspicious visitors.

---

11. See Howie, *Scots Worthies*, 121.
12. See Howie, *Scots Worthies*, 123, 131.
13. Howie, *Scots Worthies*, 130.

One day, two traveling cloth merchants came to the city gates, their horses packed with reams of cloth. The guards refused to let the merchants in. They called the magistrates, who in turn called John Welsh. They asked him whether they should let the merchants in. After praying for a while, Welsh advised the magistrates to turn the merchants away, for he feared the plague was contained in the packs of cloth on the horses. The merchants turned and went to the city of Cumnock about twenty miles away, where they entered and sold their goods.

The goods were infected, just as Welsh feared. The plague broke out immediately and killed so many people there were hardly enough living left to bury the dead.[14] After Welsh was imprisoned at Edinburgh castle, the plague did break out in Ayr. The people there came to him asking for help, but he was not permitted to leave the castle. Instead, he directed them to a godly man in their town, Hugh Kennedy, and promised them that God would hear Kennedy's prayers for Ayr. Hugh Kennedy led a prayer meeting in the city, and the plague began to decrease.[15]

The most famous incident in Welsh's life occurred while a godly young man, the heir of Lord Ochiltree, captain of the castle of Edinburgh, was staying at Welsh's house. He fell sick there and, after a long illness, died. Welsh had great affection for the man and was so grieved by his

14. See Howie, *Scots Worthies*, 124–25.
15. See Howie, *Scots Worthies*, 131.

death that he would not leave the young man's body. After twelve hours, some friends brought a coffin and attempted to put the body into it. Welsh persuaded them to wait. He stayed with the body a full twenty-four hours, praying and lamenting the man's death. Again they attempted to put the body into the coffin, but he refused to let them. They came thirty-six hours after the death of the young man, now angry with Welsh. He begged them to wait twelve more hours. But after forty-eight hours, Welsh still refused to give up the body.

Welsh's friends were beside themselves. They could not understand his strange behavior. Perhaps he thought the young man had not really died but had succumbed to some kind of epileptic fit. So the friends summoned physicians to prove to Welsh that the young man was truly dead. With their instruments, they pinched the body of the young man in various places and even twisted a bow string about the corpse's head with great force. No nerve in the body of the corpse responded at all to these measures. The physicians pronounced him dead. One last time, Welsh persuaded both friends and physicians to step into the next room for an hour or two.

Welsh fell down on the floor beside the body and begged God with all of his strength. The dead man opened his eyes and cried out to Welsh, "Oh sir, I am all whole, but my head and legs." He was restored to his life and healed of his long illness. The only ill effects he suffered were in his legs where he had been pinched by the physicians, and around his head where they had twisted the bow string. Later this young man became Lord Castlestuart, the lord of a great estate in Ireland.[16]

In addition to Wishart, Knox, and Welsh, there are numerous accounts of prophetic utterances being fulfilled among other contemporary Scottish Reformers and a group that became known as the Scottish Covenanters.[17] This was especially true of the period from 1661 to 1688, when Scottish Presbyterians were being persecuted by the Stuart regime.

Robert Bruce (1554–1631)

Robert Bruce was the leading churchman in Edinburgh in his time, and "it was largely under his influence that the Scottish Reformation found stability."[18] He was known not

---

16. See Howie, *Scots Worthies*, 132–33.

17. The term "Covenanter" refers to those who signed or supported the National Covenant (1638) and the Solemn League and Covenant (1643). These Scottish documents promoted Reformed theology and the spiritual independence of the church under the sole leadership of Jesus Christ. And they opposed the innovations that their king attempted to force on the Scottish church. Generally, the Covenanters can be identified with Presbyterian theology and church polity. In addition to the works already cited by Knox, Howie, and Fleming, see also Patrick Walker, *Six Saints of the Covenant*, 2 vols., ed. D. Hay Fleming (1724–32; repr., London: Hodder & Stoughton, 1901), and Alexander Smellie, *Men of the Covenant* (1903; repr., London: Banner of Truth, 1960).

18. Cameron, *Dictionary of Scottish Church History and Theology*, 104.

only for his prophetic ministry but for other supernatural experiences as well. One of his biographers, Robert Fleming, wrote in 1671 that even though he had well-authenticated accounts of many of Bruce's supernatural experiences, he had refrained from writing them down because they would seem so strange and marvelous.[19] He said of Bruce:

> He was one that had the spirit of discerning in a great measure. He did prophetically speak of many things which afterwards came to pass, yea, which I had attested by sober, and grave Christians, who were familiar with him. Various persons distracted [insane], and of these who were passed all hope of recovery in the falling sickness [epilepsy], were brought to Mr. Bruce and after prayer by him in their behalf were fully recovered.[20]

Robert Bruce had a healing ministry in which the insane and epileptics were completely healed. We can only wonder about the nature of the experiences that Fleming considered too supernatural to record. During this period, Fleming also mentioned angelic visitations, the audible voice of God, bright lights appearing in the darkness, physical manifestations of the Holy Spirit in meetings, and other things equally difficult for today's skeptics to believe.[21]

---

19. Fleming, *Fulfilling of the Scripture*, 430.
20. Fleming, *Fulfilling of the Scripture*, 431.
21. See Fleming, *Fulfilling of the Scripture*, 416, 418, 419, 432, 437–40.

Alexander Peden (1626–1686)

One of the most remarkable prophetic Scottish Covenanters
was Alexander Peden. His prophetic ministry was so out-
standing he was called Prophet Peden.[22] In 1682, Peden
performed the wedding ceremony for the godly couple
John Brown and Isabel Weir. After the ceremony, he told
Isabel she had gotten a good man for her husband but that
she would not enjoy him long. He advised her to prize
his company and to keep a linen burial sheet close by, for
when she least expected it, her husband would come to a
bloody end.[23]

About three years later, Peden spent the night of
April 30, 1685, at the Browns' home in Priesthill. Peden
left the house well before dawn. As he was leaving, they
heard him repeating these words to himself: "Poor woman,
a fearful morning. A dark, misty morning."[24] After Peden
had left, John Graham of Claverhouse arrived with a group
of soldiers. Graham gave John Brown an opportunity to
repent of his conviction that Christ was the head of the
church rather than King James of Scotland. Brown refused.

---

22. See Thomas Cameron, *Peden Paul* (Edinburgh: Dickson, 1981), 5.
His story is also told by Alexander Smellie in his famous book *Men of the
Covenant*, 377–89; see also 331–35 for Peden's prophecy regarding John Brown.
John Howie's *Scots Worthies*, 502–15, also contains a brief account of his life.
The fullest account is given by Walker, *Six Saints of the Covenant*, 1:45–178;
2:119–55.

23. See Howie, *Scots Worthies*, 511.

24. Smellie, *Men of the Covenant*, 332.

"Go to your prayers, for you shall immediately die," replied Graham. Brown prayed, turned to his wife Isabel, and said, "You see me summoned to appear, in a few minutes, before the court of heaven, as a witness in our Redeemer's cause, against the Ruler of Scotland. Are you willing that I should part from you?"

"Heartily willing," said Isabel. John took her into his arms, kissed her goodbye, and then kissed his baby boy. He knelt before his two-year-old daughter, kissed her, and said, "My sweet child, give your hand to God as your guide; and be your mother's comfort." When he rose, his last words were to God: "Blessed be thou, O Holy Spirit, that speaketh more comfort to my heart than the voice of my oppressors can speak terror to my ears!" Captain Graham of Claverhouse was enraged at John Brown's godly courage. He ordered six of his soldiers to shoot him where he stood. The soldiers stood motionless, refusing the order. Then Graham drew his own pistol and shot Brown through the head.

Claverhouse turned from the body of John Brown and said to Isabel, "What thinkest thou of thy husband now, woman?"

"I have always thought well of him," the widow replied, "but never more than now."[25]

The murder was committed before 7:00 a.m. By that

---

25. See John Howie, *Scots Worthies*, ed. William McGavin (1775; repr., Glasgow: McPhun, 1846), 453–56.

time, Peden was ten or eleven miles away. He entered his friend John Muirhead's house and asked to pray with the family. "Lord," he said, "when wilt Thou avenge Brown's blood? O, let Brown's blood be precious in Thy sight." He explained to the family what he had seen in a vision:

> Claverhouse has been at the Priesthill this morning, and has murdered John Brown. His corpse is lying at the end of his house, and his poor wife sitting weeping by his corpse, and not a soul to speak comfortably to her. This morning, after the sun-rising, I saw a strange apparition in the firmament, the appearance of a very bright, clear, shining star fall from heaven to the earth. And indeed there is a clear, shining light fallen this day, the greatest Christian that ever I conversed with.[26]

Meanwhile, back at Priesthill, Isabel retrieved the linen burial sheet she had reserved since the day of her wedding for this moment. With a shattered heart, she wrapped the linen around her husband's body. And though her heart was shattered, it was not shattered with bitterness. She was not bitter over wasted days in her marriage, nor was she bitter at God, or even at the enemies of God who took her husband's life. Three years before this tragic day, the word of God had come down from heaven through an old celibate

---

26. Smellie, *Men of the Covenant*, 334–35.

prophet and prepared her heart for this hour. Her heart was shattered, but it was shattered the way hearts are meant to be shattered—with love.

Sometimes I think of Isabel when people ask, "Why do we need prophets now that we have the completed Bible?"

Chapter 4

Why Bible Believers
Ignore Credible Historical
Testimony to Miracles

I spent almost twenty years in an academic theological community, and the only thing I ever heard about miracles was a monolithic denial of their existence after the apostle John died. My professors said there were only sporadic, alleged miracles in "fringe" groups with impure theology and impure character. This is what I consistently heard as a student and consistently repeated as a professor. But I lied to my students. The Scottish Covenanters and their historians were not "fringe groups with impure theology and impure character."

One of the early historians of this period, Robert Fleming (1630–1694), was a minister and theologian who was a contemporary of Alexander Peden. In 1669, he wrote *The Fulfilling of the Scripture*, in which he included an account of miraculous events during the Scottish Reformation. Fleming claimed it could not be denied that during the time of the Reformation in Scotland, God poured out a prophetic and apostolic spirit on some of his servants that did not fall short of the outpouring of his Spirit in New Testament times.[1]

---

1. See Robert Fleming, *The Fulfilling of the Scripture* (1669; repr., Rotterdam: n.p., 1671), 422–23.

Fleming and his contemporary writers should be considered credible because they saw many of these things with their own eyes. Fleming's spiritual fathers and other witnesses had passed on accounts of miracles before his time, and many of the events were a matter of public record.[2] Usually, these kinds of testimonies are considered credible historical sources. They are the kinds of sources Luke used to write his account of Jesus' ministry (Luke 1:1–4).

Fleming should also be considered credible because he was not a gullible person. He did not think prophetic revelations and miracles were the usual way of the Lord. He thought the Lord had favored Scotland with miracles during the time of Reformation because of the church's extreme need for supernatural power in overcoming the darkness that had spread across his country. He criticized those who pursued miracles and those who would rather have the Spirit work miracles than to see people saved.[3]

As for Fleming's own sincerity and character, he noted that he had been very cautious in recording these events because he judged it a "horrid" theology that would "make a lie for God."[4] He claimed not to have knowingly set down anything false and to have carefully investigated each incident. And he said he recorded only a few of the many miraculous stories that could be brought to light by anyone

---

2. See Fleming, *Fulfilling of the Scripture*, 430, 473–74.
3. See Fleming, *Fulfilling of the Scripture*, 422–23, 452, 472–73.
4. Fleming, *Fulfilling of the Scripture*, 474.

willing to make the same careful search.[5] He refused to put in his book some stories told to him by credible witnesses because he thought they were so strange that people would have trouble believing them.[6]

Yet another reason to believe these stories is that the character of the people to whom miracles and prophetic utterances were attributed is beyond question. Fleming notes that the supernatural element in their ministries never contradicted the Bible. They never pressed people to believe their revelations. They were cautious, humble, and sober people, many of whom suffered exile and imprisonment for their beliefs. Many were tortured and killed because they refused to give up their Presbyterian convictions. These people were neither flighty nor fraudulent.[7]

Fleming did not claim that the prophecies and miracles proved Presbyterian doctrine. He believed any doctrine that required a miracle to prove it was false. For his doctrine, he appealed to a higher authority than miracles—namely, the Bible.[8] His motive in writing down miraculous stories was to glorify God: "We judge it a grave and a concerning duty to observe the wondrous works of the Lord. In our times, yea, to make a diligent search thereafter, that we may tell our posterity some of the great acts of our God."[9]

---

5. See Fleming, *Fulfilling of the Scripture*, 474.
6. See Fleming, *Fulfilling of the Scripture*, 430.
7. See Fleming, *Fulfilling of the Scripture*, 423.
8. Fleming, *Fulfilling of the Scripture*, 473–74.
9. Fleming, *Fulfilling of the Scripture*, 474.

Fleming was imprisoned for his faith and died in exile from his beloved Scotland.[10] When all these things are considered together, it would be difficult to find a more credible historical witness than Fleming. But he was not the only credible witness to these events.

Samuel Rutherford (1600–1661) was a great church leader and theologian of seventeenth-century Scotland. He was one of the Scottish delegates to the famous Westminster Assembly. He knew about the ministry of John Welsh and other Scottish Presbyterians who were making prophetic utterances. Rutherford saw no necessary conflict between the authority of the Bible and God's gift of divine revelation to certain people:

> There is a revelation of some particular men, who have foretold things to come, even since the ceasing of the Canon of the word, as John Husse [John Hus], Wickeliefe [Wycliffe], Luther have foretold things to come and they certainely fell out, and in our nation of Scotland, M. George Wishart foretold that Cardinall Beaton should not come out alive at the Gates of the Castle of St. Andrewes, but that he should dye a shamefull death, and he was hanged over the window that he did look out at, when he saw the man of God burnt,

---

10. See Nigel M. de S. Cameron, ed., *Dictionary of Scottish Church History and Theology* (Edinburgh: T&T Clark, 1993), 325.

M. Knox prophesied of the hanging of the Lord of Grange, M. Ioh. Davidson uttered prophecies, knowne to many of the kingdome, diverse Holy and mortified preachers in England have done the like.[11]

Rutherford had no difficulty believing that revelation continued "even since the ceasing of the Canon." Although he was writing against the revelations of the Anabaptists, he had no difficulty accepting the prophecies and revelations of the Scottish Covenanters, as well as prophecies that came from other Reformers. The reasons he gave for accepting these prophetic revelations were:

1. They were not contradictory to the Bible.
2. They came from godly people.
3. The people who had these revelations did not claim their prophecies had the same authority as Scripture.
4. They required no one to obey their prophecies.[12]

---

11. Samuel Rutherford, *A Survey of the Spirituall Antichrist* (London: Crooke, 1648), 42. The reference to M. Ioh. Davidson is to John Davidson of Prestonpans (also called Salt-Prestoun in old documents). He was the preacher on the day that the Holy Spirit fell on the ministers in St. Giles in March 1596 and started a revival. He had been at St Andrews as a regent or master of his college in the last days of John Knox. He was known for his prophetic words (see R. Moffat Gillon, *John Davidson of Prestonpans* [London: Clarke, 1936]).

12. Rutherford, *A Survey of the Spirituall Antichrist*, 43.

Men like Rutherford and Fleming were not gullible. They were theologically astute and godly. And they witnessed many of the events they reported. These credentials make for credible historical witnesses.[13]

When I began sifting through historical records for supernatural ministry, I found not only ministries I had never heard of, but also supernatural surprises in ministries I thought I knew well, like George Whitefield's, Jonathan Edwards's, and Charles Wesley's, but none surprised me more than Charles Spurgeon's (1834–1892), the great Baptist preacher from England. Once while giving a sermon at Exeter Hall, Spurgeon suddenly stopped in the middle of his sermon and pointed to a young man, saying, "Young man, those gloves you are wearing have not been paid for.

---

13. Patrick Walker (ca. 1666–1745) published the *Life and Prophecies of Mr. Alexander Peden* in 1724. Eventually, this work was combined with the biographies of five other Scottish Covenanters and published under the title *Six Saints of the Covenant.* The edition I have was edited by D. H. Fleming and published by Hodder & Stoughton of London in 1901. Before Walker wrote Peden's biography, he traveled more than a thousand miles in Scotland and Ireland between the years 1722 and 1723, collecting facts about Peden's life. Walker was not an educated man, a fact revealed by his grammar and style. He came under heavy criticism by a contemporary chronicler of the Covenanters, Robert Wodrow (1679–1734). The attacks against Walker's accuracy were likely prompted by his poor style and his bombastic criticism of the established church rather than by real historical errors in his work. Walker's historical accuracy has stood the test of time. D. H. Fleming, who wrote the introduction to the 1901 edition of Walker's work, claimed "that a number of his marvelous stories can be corroborated from other works, some of which he never saw. His quotations are fairly accurate, and his dates are on the whole amazingly correct" (xxix). See also the positive evaluation by D. C. Lachman in *Dictionary of Scottish Church History and Theology,* ed. Cameron, 851–52. Walker was himself a Covenanter who was imprisoned and tortured for his faith.

You have stolen them from your employer." Afterward, the young man confessed to Spurgeon that he had stolen the gloves, but that he would now make restitution for his sin.[14] On another occasion while he was preaching, Spurgeon said there was a man in the gallery who had a bottle of gin in his pocket. This not only startled the man in the gallery who had the gin, but it also led to his conversion.[15]

Listen to Spurgeon's own explanation of his prophetic ministry:

> While preaching in the hall, on one occasion, I deliberately pointed to a man in the midst of the crowd, and said, "There is a man sitting there, who is a shoemaker; he keeps his shop open on Sundays, it was open last Sabbath morning, he took ninepence, and there was fourpence profit out of it; his soul is sold to Satan for fourpence!" A city missionary, when going his rounds, met with this man, and seeing that he was reading one of my sermons, he asked the question, "Do you know Mr. Spurgeon?" "Yes," replied the man, "I have every reason to know him, I have been to hear him; and, under his preaching, by God's grace I have become a new creature in Christ Jesus. Shall I tell you how it happened?

---

14. See Charles H. Spurgeon, *The Full Harvest*, vol. 2 in *C. H. Spurgeon: Autobiography* (Carlisle, PA: Banner of Truth, 1973), 60.

15. See W. Y. Fullerton, *Charles H. Spurgeon: London's Most Popular Preacher* (Chicago: Moody, 1966), 206.

"I went to the Music Hall, and took my seat in the middle of the place; Mr. Spurgeon looked at me as if he knew me, and in his sermon he pointed to me, and told the congregation that I was a shoemaker, and that I kept my shop open on Sundays; and I did, sir. I should not have minded that; but he also said that I took ninepence the Sunday before, and that there was fourpence profit; but how he should know that, I could not tell. Then it struck me that it was God who had spoken to my soul through him, so I shut up my shop the next Sunday. At first, I was afraid to go again to hear him, lest he should tell the people more about me; but afterwards I went, and the Lord met with me, and saved my soul."[16]

Spurgeon adds this comment:

I could tell as many as a *dozen* similar cases in which I pointed at somebody in the hall without having the slightest knowledge of the person, or any idea that what I said was right, except that I believed I was moved by the Spirit to say it; and so striking has been my description, that the persons have gone away, and said to their friends, "Come, see a man that told me all things that ever I did; beyond a doubt, he must have been sent of God to my soul, or else he could not have described me so exactly."

---

16. Charles H. Spurgeon, *The Autobiography of Charles Spurgeon* (Cincinnati, OH: Curtis & Jennings, 1899), 2: 226–27.

And not only so, but I have known many instances in which the thoughts of men have been revealed from the pulpit. I have sometimes seen persons nudge their neighbours with their elbow, because they had got a smart hit, and they have been heard to say, when they were going out, "The preacher told us just what we said to one another when we went in at the door."[17]

This great orator said that these supernatural revelations happened *many times* during his preaching.

These examples from Spurgeon illustrate what Paul said would happen in the church that prophesied: the secrets of unbelievers' hearts would be revealed, and they would fall on their faces worshiping God (1 Corinthians 14:24–25).

This small survey of Reformation history and Spurgeon's ministry are only the tiniest slice of the miraculous ministries that have been going on all over the church for the last twenty centuries.[18] Yet I talk to theological graduates all the time who have never heard of any of these miraculous

---

17. Spurgeon, *Autobiography*, 2:226–27, emphasis added.

18. It used to be difficult to excavate the reports of the Holy Spirit's supernatural works buried underneath centuries of neglect, but not anymore. Craig Keener, a professor of biblical studies at Asbury Seminary, has written *Miracles: The Credibility of the New Testament Accounts*, 2 vols. (Grand Rapids: Baker, 2011). It is a 1,172-page work cataloging authentic eyewitness reports of miracles from around the world for the last twenty centuries. The bibliography is 165 pages of fine print. Keener demonstrates that not only are there authentic reports of supernatural ministry throughout the entire history of the church, but that today there are hundreds of millions of credible eyewitness reports of miracles all over the world.

ministries. I used to blame this ignorance on a willful conspiracy by academics against the supernatural ministry of the Holy Spirit in post-biblical history. Although I can prove some willful suppression or distortion of the Holy Spirit's ministry by some writers, I overreacted.

In my cessationist days, neither I nor any of my seminary colleagues would have willfully suppressed or distorted the facts of history. We believed that the apostolic miracles of the Bible actually happened. They just weren't important to us anymore. Like the Old Testament dietary laws and sacrifices, the apostolic miracles had served their purpose. These miracles demonstrated that the apostles were trustworthy teachers of doctrine. We had their doctrine now in the completed New Testament, so miracles were no longer necessary. What was important was doctrine.

None of us searched historical records, looking for reliable reports of miracles. Why would we search for something we knew God stopped doing after the apostle John died?

The most popular church history text in my student days was *Christianity through the Centuries*, by Earle E. Cairns, chairman of the department of history and political science at Wheaton College.[19] In the index under "miracles" there is only one entry: "Christ's, 52, 53, 57." But he doesn't devote three pages to the miracles of Jesus. Aside from

---

19. Earle E. Cairns, *Christianity through the Centuries: A History of the Christian Church* (1954; repr., Grand Rapids: Zondervan, 1996).

brief mentions on pages 52 and 53, his treatment of Jesus' miracles consists of two bland paragraphs at the top of page 57 that total eight sentences. In a church history text of five hundred–plus pages, the miracles of the greatest miracle worker in the history of the world are relegated to two forgettable paragraphs. Before his eight-sentence discussion of the miracles of Christ, Cairns discourses on premillennialism for a page and a half. It is doctrine that is important, not miracles.

Contrast this with the way the New Testament writers present the ministry of Jesus. Luke writes:

> He went down with them and stood on a level place. A large crowd of his disciples was there and a great number of people from all over Judea, from Jerusalem, and from the coastal region around Tyre and Sidon, who had come to *hear him and to be healed of their diseases.* Those troubled by impure spirits were cured, and the people all tried to touch him, because power was coming from him and healing them all.
>
> *Luke 6:17–19, emphasis added*

The Gospels are filled with these kinds of stories because miracles played a huge role in the spread of the message that Jesus preached. Jesus even said to the Jews who refused to believe in him, "Even though you do not believe me, believe the works, that you may know and understand that the

Father is in me, and I in the Father" (John 10:38). Before Jesus raised Lazarus from the dead, he prayed that those watching would believe in him, and when Lazarus walked out of the tomb, many of those watching placed their faith in Jesus (11:41–45). But even though miracles draw an audience for the gospel, they do not guarantee faith. The religious intelligentsia never doubted that Jesus raised Lazarus from the dead, but their hearts were so hardened against God that the raising of Lazarus made them determined to kill Jesus before he took over the whole nation (11:46–53).

Earle Cairns's treatment of the apostle Paul is worse than his treatment of Jesus. Cairns doesn't mention a single miracle in the ministry of Paul. Instead, he attributes the phenomenal spread of the gospel in Paul's ministry to "Paul's genius" as a strategic church planter, writer, theologian, and polemicist.[20] I'm sure that Cairns believed in the miracles of Paul and that he did not willfully suppress them. He simply didn't think they were an important part of the expansion of the church. Paul tells a different story of his church planting:

> Therefore I glory in Christ Jesus in my service to God. I will not venture to speak of anything except what Christ has accomplished through me in leading the Gentiles to obey God by what I have *said and done*—by the power of signs and wonders, through the power of

---

20. Cairns, *Christianity through the Centuries*, 67–71.

the Spirit of God. So from Jerusalem all the way around
to Illyricum, I have fully proclaimed the gospel of Christ.

Romans 15:17–19, emphasis added

Paul writes as though signs and wonders were part of
the gospel, not a temporary sideshow. The good news is
not simply that God is here, but that God is here in power:
"The kingdom of God is not a matter of talk but of power"
(1 Corinthians 4:20).

When the Corinthians were in danger of deserting
Paul and following false teachers, he reminded them that
he did signs, wonders, and miracles among them with great
perseverance, something that the false teachers could not
do (2 Corinthians 12:12). The church at Ephesus did not
explode because Paul was a great polemicist who could
outargue the priests at the temple of Artemis. Luke wrote,
"God did extraordinary miracles through Paul, so that even
handkerchiefs and aprons that had touched him were taken
to the sick, and their illnesses were cured and the evil spirits
left them" (Acts 19:11–12).

And the same was true of the church in Jerusalem when
it exploded. The huge growth was not due to preaching
alone but to preaching with signs and wonders:

The apostles performed many signs and wonders
among the people. And all the believers used to meet
together in Solomon's Colonnade. No one else dared

join them, even though they were highly regarded by the people. Nevertheless, more and more men and women believed in the Lord and were added to their number. As a result, people brought the sick into the streets and laid them on beds and mats so that at least Peter's shadow might fall on some of them as he passed by. Crowds gathered also from the towns around Jerusalem, bringing their sick and those tormented by impure spirits, and all of them were healed.

Acts 5:12–16

I knew about the miracles of Acts, but I had no interest in them. I was interested in the speeches of Acts, the doctrine of Acts. I couldn't do miracles, but I could do theology and give talks that moved hearts.

Even though every chapter of Acts has a story of the supernatural ministry of the Holy Spirit or repeats an earlier story of the supernatural ministry of the Holy Spirit,[21] we found a way to disqualify Luke's witness. My colleagues and I taught that Acts was "descriptive," not "prescriptive."

I had memorized and taught my church 2 Timothy 3:16–17: "All Scripture is God-breathed and is useful for teaching, rebuking, correcting and training in righteousness, so that the servant of God may be thoroughly equipped for every good work." But I never saw that by calling Acts a

---

21. See appendix 1.

76

"descriptive" book, I was contradicting Scripture. According to Paul, there is no such thing as "descriptive" Scripture. All of Scripture is prescriptive, teaching us to live righteously.[22]

Another way my colleagues and I justified the absence of miracles in our churches and discarded the historical witness of Acts was to call Acts a "transitional" book, so that the Christianity of Acts does not portray "normal" Christian experience. But using this same argument from contemporary absence, we could also discard the apostle Paul's passionate devotion to Jesus Christ. How many people have you met who could truthfully say with the apostle Paul, "I do all things for the sake of the gospel" (1 Corinthians 9:23 NASB)? Or "For to me, to live is Christ" (Philippians 1:21)? I've found this kind of passion to be abnormal in the church today, but it is still the goal for all Christians.

If Acts represents abnormal Christianity when compared with the present state of the church, wouldn't we be better off to choose the abnormal experience of Acts? Isn't it a biblical principle never to be content with our experience of God but to always want more of his presence, more of his voice, more of his power? We are to be content with our material possessions (Hebrews 13:5), but we are never to be content with our present experience of God—thankful, but not content. To be content means to

---

22. See also 1 Corinthians 10:6, where Paul claims that the stories of the Old Testament were written for us as examples.

become Laodicean, lukewarm, complacent. And lukewarm believers are in danger of losing the conscious presence of God (Revelation 3:14–22).

If we say that the book of Acts represents an abnormal state of Christianity, we may be guilty of judging Scripture. When we say it is abnormal, we are comparing the experience of the New Testament church in the book of Acts to *something else we regard as normal.* Is this "something else" another scriptural history of the New Testament church? No, the book of Acts is the only inspired, inerrant account we have of the church's history. None of the histories of the church written since Acts have the same divine authority or truth. Because its ultimate author is God, the book of Acts is a perfect witness to the kind of life the early church experienced. Like the rest of Scripture, it is also a witness meant to teach us about life in God.

Luke's repeated stress on the creative ways in which the voice of God broke through every kind of barrier in every kind of circumstance to speak, warn, guide, deliver, inspire, comfort, predict, and judge ought to make us careful about calling these experiences abnormal. It could be that if we're not experiencing these things, it is *our* experience of God that is abnormal rather than the experience of the New Testament Christian.

I don't believe we should experience an unbroken chain of angelic visitations and audible voices. Even the apostles were forced to live with ambiguity and endure the silence of God. Sometimes God let an apostle die an "untimely" death as in the case of James, while he sent an angel to deliver Peter from execution (Acts 12). There will always be times when "the word of the LORD was rare; there were not many visions" (1 Samuel 3:1). No one can deny the sovereign ebb and flow between the ocean of heaven and the shores of earth. But we are better off to long for the flow rather than being content with the ebb.

If all things are possible for him who believes, and Acts shows us some of these possibilities, the Christianity of Acts should be our goal. Better yet, don't assume that Acts represents the apex of Christian experience. The Lord of history has shown us that he has saved his best wine for the last days. I want to drink that wine.

I never saw a miracle, never heard God's voice outside the Bible, until the Christianity of Acts became a model of Christian life for me. Since that turning point, I have experienced many of the same things reported in apostolic times. I know credible witnesses who have experienced more than I have.

The Christianity expressed in Acts—the passion for Jesus, the commitment to prayer and evangelism, hearing God's voice regularly, and believing God for healing and miracles—should be the goal for all churches today. Anything less really is less.

Chapter 5

Keep the Main Thing
the Main Thing

For those of us who believe in Jesus, the great difficulty in walking out our faith is to keep the main thing the main thing. There are a good many things that compete with loving Jesus and listening to his voice. When I first came to believe in Jesus, I made studying the Bible the main thing. When I first came to believe in healing and saw Jesus heal people, I made healing the main thing. Rather than being offended with me in these side trips, he used his voice in creative ways to call me back to him. Every morning, I have to pray for power to love Jesus and hear his voice, or the flow of the day will carry me away from him.

The most common way I hear the voice of Jesus is when I pray and read the Bible. Prayer is the key that unlocks the teaching ministry of the Holy Spirit. Without the enlightening ministry of the Spirit, the Bible is a dead letter (2 Corinthians 3:6–17). Without the ministry of the Spirit, knowledge of the Bible can harden the heart. This is what happened to the religious leaders of Jesus' day. They "knew" a significant amount of Scripture, but Jesus told them that they had never heard the voice of the Father. Their pride in their knowledge of Scripture kept them from coming to Jesus for spiritual life (John 5:37–39).

The anonymous psalmist, one of the greatest Scripture scholars ever, gave us a great prayer to release the power of the Word of God into our hearts. "Open thou mine eyes, that I may behold wondrous things out of thy law" (Psalm 119:18 KJV). I was a kid newly come to Christ, rummaging around the psalms in my King James Bible, not even knowing what a psalm was, when the beauty of this prayer dazzled me. I've prayed it ever since, and I have never been able to give up the Elizabethan language for this verse.

The New Testament illustration of God showing us wondrous things out of Scripture is found in the story of those two depressed disciples walking to Emmaus after the crucifixion. They had lost their confidence in Jesus to do what he said he would do, thinking he was dead and gone forever. Suddenly Jesus walked beside them, but they were prevented from recognizing him. Jesus gave them the remedy for their depression by "beginning with Moses and all the Prophets, he explained to them what was said in all the Scriptures concerning himself" (Luke 24:27). The greatest sermon ever preached was preached by the Son of God. The subject was the Son of God. The text was the entire Old Testament. It lasted all day. And only two people heard it.

At dinner that evening, they recognized Jesus, and he vanished from their sight. They said, "Were not our hearts burning within us while he talked with us on the road and opened the Scriptures to us?" (Luke 24:32). Jesus could have revealed himself as soon as he met them, but he didn't. He was showing them and all his family to come after them that the primary way he will meet us is by revealing himself to us in his written Word. It is not the only way he reveals himself or speaks to us, but for me it is the primary way I meet him.

When I open the Bible, I pray, "Open thou mine eyes that I may behold wondrous things out of thy law." Then I imagine my Teacher sitting beside me, and I try to put my hand in his hand in hopes that my heart will burn with his beauty. Sometimes it does.

For the first twenty years of my walk with Jesus, I connected with God primarily through reading and studying the Bible. Prayer was important to me, not as the superlative way of communing with God, but as the main tool for opening up the meaning of Scripture. I failed to understand the implications of the fact that the Holy Spirit and the Son of God are praying for us nonstop.

> In the same way, the Spirit helps us in our weakness. We do not know what we ought to pray for, but the Spirit himself intercedes for us through wordless groans. And he who searches our hearts knows the mind of the Spirit, because the Spirit intercedes for God's people in accordance with the will of God.
>
> *Romans 8:26–27[1]*

---

1. The one who searches the hearts and minds of the saints is Jesus (Revelation 2:23).

Who then is the one who condemns? No one. Christ Jesus who died—more than that, who was raised to life—is at the right hand of God and is also interceding for us.

Romans 8:34

Therefore he is able to save completely those who come to God through him, because he always lives to intercede for them.

Hebrews 7:25

If the second and third persons of the Trinity never cease praying, how much more important is it for a weak, inconsistent person like me to pray? Jesus taught his disciples to follow his example of always praying. Just before the crucifixion, Jesus said to the Twelve:

Be careful, or your hearts will be weighed down with carousing, drunkenness and the anxieties of life, and that day will close on you suddenly like a trap. For it will come on all those who live on the face of the whole earth. Be always on the watch, and pray that you may be able to escape all that is about to happen, and that you may be able to stand before the Son of Man.

Luke 21:34–36

Jesus looked at his A-team, his most committed followers, and said, "Peter, you are the rock, but if you don't pray, carousing will take you down, and you will waste your life on the pursuit of pleasure. John, you're my best friend, but if you don't pray, you will become a drunk. All of you, pray or the anxieties of life will steal your reward." It is this warning that has caused me to see prayer as the most important thing I do.

God governs the world through the prayers of his saints. When we pray, "Our Father in heaven, hallowed be your name, your kingdom come" (Matthew 6:9–10), we have a part in causing God's name to be honored on the earth and a part in hastening the coming of his kingdom to the earth (see also 2 Peter 3:12). When I pray, the Lord often speaks to me even when I'm not asking him a question, like he spoke to Peter when Peter went up on Simon's roof simply to pray without realizing that God was about to use him to open the door of the kingdom to the Gentiles (Acts 10:9–16).

A few years ago, when Leesa was incapacitated by an illness, I did all the housework and cooking. One morning after I made our breakfast, Leesa watched a cooking show. I asked her if I could switch the TV to a news channel for ten minutes while I finished my breakfast, but she refused. I thought, *Is this the thanks I get for cleaning the house and making your breakfast?* But I kept my expression neutral as I walked into my study. I sat down at my desk and put on my headphones to calm myself. I listened to Beethoven and grew angrier. *Leesa can be so selfish*, I thought. I tried to write, but I couldn't. My anger grew. I prayed, "Lord please help me." I opened the Bible to take my mind off the injustice inflicted on me. I turned to a story I knew by heart—Jesus raising Lazarus from the dead in John 11. I expected nothing from the story. I was only trying to let my anger drain away.

I came to the verse where Martha said to Mary, "The Teacher is here and is asking for you." My heart exploded with wonder. The infinite One who has no needs asked for the little one simply because he wanted to be with her. Then I saw a vision of Jesus looking down on me, sideswiped by self-righteous anger at my invalid wife. He turned to his left and said, "Father, let me have Jack for a few minutes. I'll call him to John 11 and bring him back to us." Then I wept to the strains of the *Moonlight Sonata*. I went from feeling wronged to feeling desired by infinite love. All I did was open my Bible and take my bad attitude to Jesus, and he turned it into worship.

I have these kinds of experiences with the Lord often now.

In the first twenty years of my walk with Jesus, I can't remember a single visionary experience like the one I just described, even though I read the Bible and prayed regularly. Back then, I preached against "legalists," but my self-esteem rose and fell with the uneven nature of my obedience to God. I believed that one day, I would do better because I knew better. But better never showed up.

I said, "I know God loves me," but secretly I felt he was disappointed in the quality of my service. *I* was disappointed in the quality of my service.

For more than twenty years, I had stood on stages and hurled obligations at my followers without giving them a Person to enjoy. At my seminary, we were fond of saying that we preach the word of God, not our experience. But that is a lie. All preachers preach their experience. I hurled obligations at my church because that is how I experienced God. I defined loving God as obeying God. I supported this with the words of Jesus: "If you love me, keep my commands" (John 14:15). I did not believe that God spoke outside the pages of Scripture, so my experience of God loving me was confined to scriptural statements of his love, like John 3:16. In those first twenty years, I can't recall a single experience of God *showing* me he loved me in all my weaknesses and impurity. I thought that obeying God exhausted what it meant to love God.

I had locked God into his Bible.

Then he sent prophets to me, and I began to hear his voice outside the Bible.

It's funny how you can read a verse of Scripture hundreds of times without that verse ever leaving the page. It just lies there as lifeless as the paper on which it is printed. But then one magical day, it springs off the page and finds a home in your heart and fills you with hope by the power of the Holy Spirit.

Jesus said, "I no longer call you servants, because a servant does not know his master's business. Instead, I have called you friends, for everything that I learned from my Father I have made known to you" (John 15:15).[2] The essence of friendship is not service, but pleasure. We have a best friend for the pleasure it gives us to be with our best friend. We experience a joy when we are with our best friend that we don't experience with anyone else. And out of the soil of that joy grows a commitment to our best friend that we don't have to anyone else. We can share our secrets, our fears, our worst traits with our best friend and feel relief because we know that our best friend will pray for us and never betray our confidence. A counselor once told me, "If you can't talk about it, *it* owns you." When we tell our friend the secret we think makes us unlovable and we see only love in our friend's face, the power of a dark lie is broken over us. Sure, we'll serve our best friend when needed, but that's not what the friendship is about.[3]

---

2. Jesus wasn't telling the apostles that they would no longer be servants, but that he was taking their service to a new level. From now on, they would first be his friends, who also served him. For years, I used this verse to say that Jesus wanted an "intimate" relationship with us, but I never defined *intimate* and never pondered what it meant to be his friend.

3. The most insightful essay I've ever read on friendship is by C. S. Lewis (*The Four Loves* [New York: Harcourt, Brace & World, 1960]). I first read it when I was in high school, and I can't count the number of times I've reread it. The friendship essay is on pages 87–127. Lewis argued that friendship is the primary instrument through which God reveals beauty to us, and in the revealing of beauty, he increases the beauty we see in our friends (126). My best friendships have brought me closer to God, making me a better person.

When prophets came into my life, I heard Jesus say, "I want to be your friend." And for the first time, I felt his pleasure in me, his smile instead of his sigh. He was no longer an obligation but a friend to enjoy.

For a long time, I prayed that God would grant me grace to love him with all my heart, with all my soul, with all my mind, and with all my strength, and grant me grace to love my neighbor as myself. When John 15:15 found a home in my heart, I understood for the first time that the key to fulfilling the greatest commandment lies in first feeling the love of God for me. The apostle John wrote, "We love because he first loved us" (1 John 4:19). So my first prayer of the day became, "Father, let me feel your affection today."

A wilderness lies between knowing God loves us and feeling his love for us. When I was a Young Life leader, high school boys stared at the ground when they said to me, "I know my father loves me." I thought, *If that's true, why are you so sad when you say that sentence?* They had a theoretical knowledge of their father's love but so little experience of it.

I hear that same forlorn confession all the time in the church today. The Christian who stares at the ground and says in a sad voice, "I know God loves me," is still living under the power of the lie that our value to God lies in our service. For a long time, I increased my hearers' pain by hurling obligations at them instead of offering them a Person to enjoy.

91

Today I stand on stages and tell people stories of my experiences of God's affection. I give them scriptural prayers to pray to feel God's love. Ephesians 3:16–19 is one of my daily prayers:

> I pray that out of his glorious riches he may strengthen you with power through his Spirit in your inner being, so that Christ may dwell in your hearts through faith. And I pray that you, being rooted and established in love, may have power, together with all the Lord's holy people, to grasp how wide and long and high and deep is the love of Christ, and to know this love that surpasses knowledge—that you may be filled to the measure of all the fullness of God.

I love the metaphor of being "rooted and established in love," not *our* love for God, but *God's* love for us. When I feel God's love for me, I am like a tree with deep roots in the soil of his love, and the storms of life can't knock me down. Or I am like a building built on the solid foundation of his love for me that can offer shelter to others when disaster strikes. This is not a love experienced in isolation, but in the body of Christ with other believers. God's love for us is not something we can come to by ordinary knowledge, by simply reading about it. It has to be revealed to us by the power of the Spirit.

I pray throughout the day to feel God's affection for me.

I wouldn't say I feel his affection every day, but it would be rare to go very long without some experience in which I feel his pleasure in me.

I try to begin the day by praying and meditating. I want to have pleasure in my mornings of prayer and meditation, but it doesn't always work out that way. A few years ago, I was so bored in my morning prayer that it felt like I was reciting a shopping list to God. It seemed like I was only getting a religious exercise out of the way so I could go on with my real life. I stopped, looked up to heaven, and said, "God, are you enjoying this? Because I'm not. Is this dry prayer really important to you?" I meant it as real question, but he didn't answer me. I finished my list.

My son is a journalist, and I pray daily for his writing.

Three days later, my son Stephen called me in the morning during my prayer time. At the end of the conversation, he said, "Oh, Dad, I just won best feature writer in the state of Missouri again." Before I could say, "Wonderful!" I heard God say, "Is this really important to you?"

He is so creative in the way he shows us his love and answers our questions.

The Lord is so merciful that he is not offended by our dry prayers. A famous old revivalist whom I came to know and admire at the end of his race used to say, "God doesn't answer prayer. He answers desperate prayer." And my friend did pray with a great deal of emotion that seemed sincere to me. But Scripture does not teach that God only answers desperate prayers; Scripture teaches that God answers persistent prayers (Luke 11:5–8; 18:1–8; Acts 1:14; Romans 1:9–10; 12:12; Colossians 4:2, 12; 1 Thessalonians 5:17). In my experience, praying every day requires a great deal of faith and perseverance without adding the burden of conjuring up emotion.

It became easier to pray daily when I learned that God wanted to be my friend as well as my Lord. Friends talk to each other. It gives God pleasure to tell us and show us he loves us. He also speaks to us because we need his guidance to fulfill his highest purposes for our lives, just as Jesus did, just as the apostles did, and just as all his friends in the New Testament did.

Chapter 6

What God Reveals
to His Children

For the first seventeen years of my life, I wanted nothing to do with God or Jesus or church. I saw no beauty or love in God, only his demand that I satisfy him by living an incredibly dull life. Everything I wanted or enjoyed, he forbade. I saw nothing attractive in his church kids. At 2:00 a.m. on December 18, 1965, I heard for the first time that Jesus Christ died on the cross for me and that if I would trust him to forgive my sins and give me a new life, he would come into my heart and never leave. My response was immediate. Before I could debate the consequences and count the cost of the pleasures I'd have to give up and the friends I'd have to lose, my first prayer was on its way up to the throne of God. It was a silent prayer, a simple, short declarative sentence: "God, I'm comin' over to your side now."

I had been born again. My prayer was the result of my new birth. But I did not know that. This fatherless boy now had a Father who had already begun to make wrong things right in his new kid's life. But I did not know that. One minute I was headed to hell, and then, in a single beat of my heart, I was on my way to that seat reserved for me in heaven before the beginning of time. What caused me to pray that prayer?

God Reveals His Beauty
to His Children

According to Jesus, the primary ministry of the Holy Spirit is to reveal the beauty of Jesus (John 15:26). It begins at our conversion and lasts for the rest of our lives. Once the Holy Spirit showed me the beauty of Jesus' love for me, life without him was no longer a possibility for me. The Holy Spirit delights to reveal the excellencies of God, and then we have the privilege of telling the stories of our experience of the beauty of God to others (1 Peter 2:9). Heaven is not a static enjoyment of God; it is a never-ending journey into the perfections of an infinite Person. The revelation of God's beauty will continue for all eternity, for his beauty is infinite. The joy of heaven is seeing the beauty of God and then praising him for that revelation. It is like being in love forever with an ever-increasing ecstasy.

The Holy Spirit Guides Us in
All the Details of Our Lives

In the upper room, Jesus promised his eleven disciples that the Holy Spirit "will guide you into all the truth" (John 16:13). Three of the Eleven would go on to write Scripture, and this promise guarantees the veracity of Scripture, but it should not be restricted to the writing of

Scripture or to the lives of the Eleven. The Holy Spirit was sent to lead the lives of *all* the children of God (Romans 8:14; Galatians 5:18).

The Holy Spirit shows us what our gifts and ministries are (Acts 13:2), and then he gives specific directions in our ministries (Acts 16:6–10; Galatians 2:1–2). Sometimes he will give us warnings to save us from traps (Job 33:13–17; Acts 22:17–21). Sometimes the Spirit will speak to us when we are afraid and give us the encouragement we need to finish a task to which he has called us (Acts 18:9–11).

The Holy Spirit Shows Us How to Apply Scripture

When I was a seminary student, I fell in love with the Servant Songs of Isaiah (42:1–9; 49:1–7; 50:4–9; 52:13–53:12). They progressively reveal the beauty, sufferings, and victory of the Messiah, who is portrayed as an anonymous suffering servant of Yahweh. The first song describes the humility and gentleness of the Messiah when he comes: "A bruised reed he will not break, and a smoldering wick he will not snuff out" (42:3). This magnificent metaphor shows how Jesus would love the downtrodden who despaired of life. Many years later, on a Sunday morning, I stood at the front of the sanctuary at John Wimber's church. I was the leader of the prayer teams. About a hundred people had come to the front for prayer. I overheard a woman on our prayer team being a little too forceful with the woman she was praying for. I walked over to her to correct her, waiting until she finished praying for the woman. Before I could correct her, the verse that had lain hidden in my heart for a quarter century—"A bruised reed he will not break, and a smoldering wick he will not snuff out"—entered my mind as I looked at the overbearing woman. God was telling me she was a bruised reed and that on this Sunday morning, all it would take to crush her was a corrective word from a pastor she esteemed. I smiled at her and moved on. The Spirit not only gives us understanding of Scripture (Psalm 119:18); he also shows us how to apply Scripture so that we heal instead of bruise his people.

The Holy Spirit Reveals Our Sins

One of the most frequent ways the Holy Spirit leads me to experience the love of God is by showing me my sin. I need God to reveal my sins to me because they are so characteristic, so ingrained within me, that sometimes I can't even see the worst of them. The great saints always asked God to reveal their sins. David prayed, "Search me, God, and know my heart; test me and know my anxious thoughts. See if there is any offensive way in me, and lead me in the way everlasting" (Psalm 139:23–24).

The great saints not only pray for God to reveal their sin; they also claim to be the greatest sinners. Psalm 119 is the greatest psalm ever written on the power and beauty of the Scripture. It was written by an incomparable but anonymous poet. It is 176 verses long. Throughout the hymn, the psalmist displays his love for God:

> I seek you with all my heart;
> > do not let me stray from your commands.
> I have hidden your word in my heart
> > that I might not sin against you. (vv. 10–11)

> My eyes stay open through the watches of
> > the night,
> > that I may meditate on your promises. (v. 148)

Throughout the psalm, it is clear that the psalmist is suffering and that God has not answered his prayer to save him from his pain. Instead of complaining about God's indifference, he celebrates the wisdom of God:

> It was good for me to be afflicted
> > so that I might learn your decrees. (v. 71)

The psalmist, who is a model of godliness in every way, ends his hymn with this verse:

> I have strayed like a lost sheep.
>
> Seek your servant,
>
> for I have not forgotten your commands.
>
> (v. 176)

This confession can't be attributed to modesty or, worse, to false humility. The poet is writing Scripture under the direction of the Holy Spirit. He can only write what is true. How could such a godly person consider himself a lost sheep that has strayed away from God? The most graphic example of this kind of confession is found in the apostle Paul. What Paul wrote is so troubling to some biblical scholars, theologians, and preachers that they explain away the plain meaning of his words. At the end of his life, Paul wrote, "Here is a trustworthy saying that deserves full acceptance: Christ Jesus came into the world to save sinners—of whom I am the worst" (1 Timothy 1:15).

When Paul called himself "the chief of sinners" (KJV), he seemed to contradict what he wrote earlier: "To me, to live is Christ and to die is gain" (Philippians 1:21). This "discrepancy" has led some to claim that Paul meant he "was" the chief of sinners because of his persecution of Christians before he became a Christian. The problem with this interpretation is that Paul was a superb grammarian who knew the difference between the past and present tenses. Paul used the most emphatic way of expressing the present tense in New Testament Greek. He was using the grammar to shout, "Make no mistake about it, I *am* the chief of sinners!" When we consider his history, we can see exactly what he meant.

When Paul began his walk with Jesus, he was a self-righteous, legalistic Pharisee who considered himself superior to just about everyone (Galatians 1:13–14; Philippians 3:4–6). Feeling superior to almost everyone had been ingrained into Paul all his life. That attitude is not something that goes away quickly or easily. The generally accepted date for Paul's conversion, his encounter with Jesus on the Damascus road, is AD 35. Fourteen years later (AD 49), he wrote his letter to the Galatian churches. He referred to his second visit to Jerusalem when he met with the leaders of the church to show them the version of the gospel that he preached to the Gentiles. He writes, "As for those who seemed to be important—whatever they were makes no difference to me; God does not judge by external appearance—those men added nothing to my message . . . James, Peter and John, those reputed to be pillars, gave me . . . the right hand of fellowship" (Galatians 2:6, 9 NIV 1984).

James was the Lord's brother. Peter and John were the two apostles closest to Jesus during his earthly ministry. To say that these three "seemed" to be leaders who contributed nothing to Paul's message and that they were only "reputed" to be pillars of the church, is rude and arrogant, and it shows that Paul had not yet put to death that pharisaical superiority. But Paul had only been walking with the Lord for about fourteen years when he belittled three of God's greatest servants. Personality changes slowly if it changes at all.

Give Paul another six years of walking with the Lord and suffering for him, and his attitude improved. In AD 55, he wrote to the Corinthian church, "Then he appeared to James, then to all the apostles, and last of all he appeared to me also, as to one abnormally born. For *I am the least of all the apostles* and do not deserve to be called an apostle, because I persecuted the church of God" (1 Corinthians 15:7–9, emphasis added). After walking with the Lord for twenty years, these verses show a fundamental change in Paul's personality. He was becoming humble.

Give him another seven years of walking with Jesus and suffering greatly, and we see an even more massive change in his character. He wrote to the Ephesian church in AD 62, "I became a servant of this gospel by the gift of God's grace given me through the working of his power. Although *I am less than the least of all the Lord's people*, this grace was given me: to preach to the Gentiles the boundless riches of Christ" (Ephesians 3:7–8, emphasis added).

After walking with the Lord for twenty-seven years, Paul seemed to have lost his self-righteous superiority. At the end of his life, he confessed to his spiritual son Timothy that he was not only the least of the saints, but that he had come to see himself as the chief of sinners.

Paul began his spiritual life blinded by the light. But he kept walking toward the light all his life. He was like someone in a dimly lit room who believes the room to be clean. The closer he came to the light, the dirtier the room looked. At the end of his life, he was so close to the light that he saw the rats scurrying. I can't imagine any of us wouldn't feel like the chief of sinners if we were as close to Jesus as Paul was. The greatest saints confess to being the greatest sinners because they are the closest to the glory of absolute perfection in the person of Jesus.

One of the main ways I can tell I'm growing spiritually is when I have an increasing awareness of my distance from Jesus. Not an increasing distance, but an increasing *awareness* of my distance. This can only happen when this awareness is coupled with an increasing feeling of his affection for me. This double blessing means I am moving closer to the Lord.

Years ago, I developed the habit of beginning my morning prayers by asking God to show me my sin (Psalm 139:23–24). Sometimes before I finished my prayer, he would show me someone I had refused to forgive. Sometimes he would replay a scene from the day before to show me how heartless I had been to Leesa or to one of the kids. Sometimes it would take years before I could see how cruel I had been to a dear friend who was no longer a friend. Sometimes I wept over my hard-hearted sinfulness. Sometimes I cried tears of joy because every revelation of my sins came with the affection of God. I felt so loved and special to God. When he reveals sin to his children, he always sends hope by the power of the Holy Spirit that he will enable us to change.

About eight years ago, I was skimming through the gospel of Matthew before my morning prayers. I ran into a roadblock at the Lord's Prayer (Matthew 6:9–13). The Lord confronted me about a secret I had never told anyone: I didn't like the Lord's Prayer. I refused to pray it. In my early walk with Jesus, I felt like this prayer was used in a hollow, liturgical way that failed to engage the heart or the mind. That morning I tried to justify my dislike of his prayer. I said, "Lord, why should I pray for your kingdom to come? It's going to come, whether I pray for it or not."

"True," he said, "but if you don't pray for it to come, you won't have done your part in helping my kingdom to come, and I won't be able to reward you for it."

From that day on, I have begun my morning prayers with the Lord's Prayer. I had other objections to this prayer, but I prayed the prayer anyway. I never liked the request for daily bread. It was too spartan for me. I'm more of a Cabernet and steak guy. And I never liked the first-person plural "our." I wanted to say "my" Father, "my" daily bread. I didn't want others invading my morning prayer.

One day, at the moment I prayed, "Give us today our daily bread," I fell into a vision. I was "taken" to Ethiopia.

I looked down and saw a poor, godly grandmother caring for her orphaned grandchildren. The Lord said, "I'm feeding her and her family today because you prayed for *our* daily bread." I wept and wept, and I shook. I wept over the power of a single, unemotional prayer to travel around the world and feed a hurting family. I wept over being a part of the most majestic body in the world. I wept over the beauty and wisdom of how the Lord governs the world through the prayers of his saints. But mostly I wept over feeling loved by my Lord, feeling so special that he let me in on one of his secrets in spite of my stubbornness.

"Our Father in heaven, hallowed be your name." I never knew how much I needed this particular prayer until I started daily praying for God's name to be honored in the world. Frequently during my prayers, my mind strays to a meeting I will have later in the day. I imagine what I will say to my friend. In the conversation, I am winning the argument or stunning my friend with my insight. I see awe in my friend's eyes, and I feel pleasure. During one of these little mid-prayer reveries, the Lord pointed out what I was doing. With my will I prayed for God's name to be honored, but with my heart I delighted in *my* name being honored. The Lord interrupted these self-gratulatory scenes often enough to show me how much I want to be thought of as the smartest and most spiritual person in the room.

The other day, I prayed, "Our Father in heaven, hallowed be *my* name." That little slip of the tongue demonstrated how deeply embedded in me is the desire for human praise. Instead of beating myself up—as if that would do any good—I smiled and said, "Thank you, Lord." More and more these days, the Lord is showing me how much I desire my glory, not to push me away, but to draw me in and heal me with his love. Right now, I think this is my biggest sin, but I wouldn't know it was there if God weren't speaking to me about it. He is speaking to me about it because he wants to have bragging rights over me when I finally come before the judgment seat of Christ. He wants to have the pleasure of saying to me, "Well done, good and faithful servant! You have been faithful with a few things; I will put you in charge of many things. Come and share your master's happiness!" (Matthew 25:21). This commendation is the crown of righteousness that the Lord awards to his fruitful children. They will wear it forever. It will grow heavier and greater throughout their stay in heaven, because the understanding of the greatness of the One who gave it will grow larger forever and ever. Heaven will be an infinite revelation of the beauty of Jesus.

I don't know if I'll ever have the pleasure and honor of hearing Jesus say, "Well done." But I know for certain that if all I had were my knowledge of Scripture and my discipline, I would never have a chance to hear those great words. Although Scripture can tell me that it's wrong to desire self-glory, it can never show me that I'm desiring self-glory. Only the voice can show me that. Scripture can tell me that God loves his children, but only the voice can let me feel his love. God speaks to us regularly because we need his guidance, but also because it gives him pleasure to wrap our hearts in his love.

Chapter 7

Theophanies and Angels

Throughout Scripture, God speaks to his people many times and in many ways. I'm not concerned with the unique examples like speaking to Moses through the burning bush (Exodus 3) or to Balaam through his donkey (Numbers 22), but with the repeatable ways he speaks throughout the Bible.

The Appearances of God to His People

The most spectacular way God speaks to his people is by appearing to them. He created Adam face-to-face as he breathed into his nostrils the breath of life (Genesis 2:7). After Adam and Eve sinned, they hid from God in the garden. They heard his footsteps when he came to confront them (Genesis 3:8), and presumably the whole confrontation occurred face-to-face.

The Lord appeared to Abraham (Genesis 17:1–22; 18:1–33), to Isaac (Genesis 26:2–5), and to Jacob (Genesis 32:22–32; 35:9–15). God probably appeared to and spoke to Moses more than anyone else in the Old Testament, for Moses was the mediator of the old covenant. God spoke to Moses "face to face, as one speaks to a friend" (Exodus 33:11).

One may think the Lord only appeared to important leaders, but that isn't the case. When Sarai mistreated her Egyptian maidservant Hagar so severely that Hagar ran out into the desert, God appeared to Hagar (Genesis 16:1–14) and sent her back to Sarai. God appeared to Hagar as "the angel of the LORD," the normal way he appeared to people in the Old Testament times. We know the angel of the Lord is God, for Scripture says, "She gave this name to the LORD who spoke to her: 'You are the God who sees me'" (Genesis 16:13). The angel of the Lord can be seen, so he can't be God the Father. He must be the preincarnate Christ. In other appearances, the angel of the Lord will speak of himself as God (see Genesis 22:12).

Jacob said, "I saw God face to face, and yet my life was spared" (Genesis 32:30). But God said to Moses, "You cannot see my face, for no one may see me and live" (Exodus 33:20). Later Scripture also affirms this truth (John 1:18; 1 John 4:12). So when God appeared to people in the Old Testament, it couldn't be God the Father; it must have been God the Son before his incarnation.

Theologians refer to these appearances of God as "theophanies," which is simply combining two Greek words—*theos* ("God") and *phainein* ("cause to appear").

The Greek expression isn't any more precise, but it makes us professional Christians sound more profound.

A major change comes with Joshua. The law of Moses, the Pentateuch, was completed, and the Lord required Joshua to meditate on the law day and night, for his success depended on his faithfulness to the law (Joshua 1:8). The translation of *Torah* as "law" is unfortunate. It is actually "instruction" in how to walk closely with God and how to love his people in the different situations of life. It is one of God's greatest gifts to his people, but it does not cancel their need to hear his voice, because the Torah doesn't cover all the circumstances of life. Joshua was devasted when the inferior army of Ai routed the Israelites. He thought God had abandoned him. Then the Lord spoke to Joshua, telling him the secret sin of one of the soldiers that had caused the Israelite defeat (Joshua 7:10–15). The Lord continued to speak to Joshua even though the Torah was complete. The Lord even expected the leaders to inquire of him when they encountered situations not covered in the Torah (Joshua 9:14–15). So right from the beginning of the giving of the Torah, it is made clear that Scripture did not render the voice obsolete.

In the New Testament, John reaffirmed that no one has seen God the Father, but that Jesus is God the Son who perfectly reveals the Father (John 1:1–18; 1 John 4:12). In the place of the pillar of cloud and the pillar of fire that led the Israelites in the wilderness (Exodus 13), the miracles of Jesus manifested the glory and presence of the Father. Paul said that the resurrected Christ appeared to more than five hundred people before he ascended to heaven to be glorified at the Father's side. Twenty years after the cross, the majority of those five hundred were still alive (1 Corinthians 15:6).

One or two years after the resurrection of Jesus, Saul the Pharisee was on his way to Damascus to imprison the followers of Jesus. At noon, in an explosion of light, Jesus appeared to Saul, blinded him, and knocked him to the ground, and asked him, "Saul, Saul, why do you persecute me?"

Saul asked, "Who are you, Lord?"

"I am Jesus, whom you are persecuting. Now get up and go into the city, and you will be told what you must do."[1]

This was Saul's first lesson about the body of Christ. To persecute a Christian is to persecute Christ himself. Paul was blind for three days. The Lord sent Ananias to pray for Saul to receive his sight and be filled with the Holy Spirit. Jesus showed Saul that he would grant him grace to take the gospel before Gentile kings and to suffer greatly for the name of Jesus (Acts 9:1–19).

Paul returned to Jerusalem and was in the temple praying when Jesus appeared to him again, warning him to leave Jerusalem or the Jews would kill him (Acts 22:17–21).

---

1. Acts 9:4–6.

When Paul was brought before the Sanhedrin, a violent crowd tried to tear him to pieces. That night, "the Lord stood near Paul and said, 'Take courage! As you have testified about me in Jerusalem, so you must also testify in Rome'" (23:11).

When the apostle John was in his nineties in exile on the island of Patmos, Jesus appeared to him, took him up to heaven, and commissioned him to write "the revelation from Jesus Christ" (Revelation 1:1, 9–11).

I would not say the appearances of Jesus are rare. From the beginning of time to our present age, he has consistently appeared to people. But I think an appearance is the rarest way that Jesus speaks to his followers. The appearances often come at a low point in our lives or when God is doing something new and difficult to believe in.

The Lord has never appeared to me, but he has appeared to Leesa twice. The first time, Leesa was alone in the bedroom of our Montana home, sitting in a chair looking out on the mountains and calling out to the Lord. She was in despair. The atmosphere in the room changed. She felt a presence coming up behind her. She knew Jesus was in the room, but she was so terrified that she couldn't turn around. She closed her eyes. He seemed to be beside her on her right. She opened her eyes and stared at the floor. She saw his feet in sandals and the bottom of his cream-colored robe. Then she felt his hand on her right shoulder. He spoke to her what she most needed to hear, and then he vanished.

The second time was a year after we lost our son Scott. This time it was a face-to-face encounter. Angels took her up to heaven. Jesus comforted her with words about Scott, and then he gave us an assignment for the future we have yet to fulfill. Then the angels brought her back to our home. After it was over, Leesa said, "If I could look into his face for all eternity, I would be perfectly happy. I wouldn't want anything else. It was that wonderful. Whenever I feel guilty about something, I think about Jesus' face, and the guilt lifts."

Leesa is not the only person I know who has seen the Lord. Over the years, friends I know well, and others I do not know so well, have told me credible stories of the Lord appearing to them.

Our Protection against Deception

A note of caution here. Paul warned the Corinthians:

> Such people are false apostles, deceitful workers, masquerading as apostles of Christ. And no wonder, for Satan himself masquerades as an angel of light. It is not surprising, then, if his servants also masquerade as servants of righteousness. Their end will be what their actions deserve.
>
> *2 Corinthians 11:13–15*

The apostle Paul knew that Satan and his demons could deceive us by appearing as angels or by imitating the voice of God. He also knew that our desire to exalt ourselves in the church could lead us into false visions and impressions (Colossians 2:16–19). He knew that even true apostles could be carried away by hypocrisy so that they compromised the truth of the gospel (Galatians 2:11–21). When we refuse to forgive (2 Corinthians 2:5–11), when we pursue something more than we pursue Jesus, or when we fear people more than God, we are in danger of deception.

The reality is that at one time or another, all of us will be deceived. I was deceived for almost twenty years. I taught my students and my church that God no longer healed, and he no longer spoke except in Scripture. Neither assertion was based on Scripture. They were based on pride and fear. I was more afraid of Satan's ability to deceive me than the Holy Spirit's ability to lead me. I was a perfectionist who was proud of my knowledge of Scripture and my skill in the biblical languages. I used that knowledge to exalt myself. My worst deception was taking no real risks for God and thinking myself superior to most people. Now I know it is the perfectionists who do the most damage in the body of Christ.

The apostle Paul never allowed the danger of deception to impede his passionate pursuit of the supernatural. He told us to earnestly pursue spiritual gifts, especially prophesying (1 Corinthians 14:1). We have the Spirit of God, the gift of discernment, the fellowship of spiritual believers, and the Scriptures to help protect us from deception. The believers who pursue God passionately make mistakes and learn from them.

Angels

It used to be common for people to think that angels and demons were the ghosts of departed dead people.[2] Even today, I hear grown-ups comfort children who have lost a loved one by saying, "Honey, God just needed another angel." I flinch every time I hear a child lulled into false comfort with this deception.

Angels are supernatural spiritual beings who serve the purposes of God. They were created before time and sang for joy at the creation of the earth (Job 38:6–7). They are an innumerable army of God (Hebrews 12:22; Revelation 5:11). As in any army, angels vary in authority, power, and function. Before the creation of the earth, a powerful angel led a rebellion against God. Revelation 12:4 may mean that this angel, whose name became Satan, "the adversary," led

---

2. One of the most graphic stories of demonic deliverance I have ever read is that of Pastor Johann Blumhardt's casting multiple demons out of Gottliebin Dittus, a single twenty-eight-year-old woman in 1842 in the Black Forest in Germany. The demons claimed to be the spirits of wicked dead people, a common belief among Christians at the time (see *Blumhardt's Battle: A Conflict with Satan* [New York: Lowe, 1970], 20).

as many as one-third of the angelic army away from God. These fallen angels became demons. They are 100 percent committed to evil. Ever since this rebellion, God has allowed a cosmic war to proceed between his angels and the demons (Daniel 10:12–14; Revelation12:7–12). When Jesus returns, he will cast Satan and the demons into eternal punishment (Matthew 25:41).

Although different classes of angels are mentioned, like seraphim and cherubim, no one really knows how many different kinds there are. The apostles John and Paul both were taken up into heaven but were forbidden to tell some of the things they saw and heard. Heaven has its secrets. There will always be only one omniscient Being.

Angels may do their work without being seen, or they may appear in terrifying glory as they did when they announced and celebrated the birth of Jesus (Luke 2:8–14). Angels cared for Jesus after the devil tempted him (Matthew 4:11), and an angel strengthened him in his agony the night before the crucifixion (Luke 22:43).

Angel both in Hebrew and Greek means "messenger." Angels reveal the plans of God. Gabriel told Zechariah that Elizabeth would give birth to the forerunner of the Messiah, and he told Mary she would give birth to the Messiah (Luke 1–2). Twice an angel broke Peter out of jail (Acts 5 and 12). An angel sent Cornelius to Peter to hear the gospel (Acts 10), and an angel sent Philip to the Gaza road to present the gospel to the Ethiopian eunuch (Acts 8:26–40).

An angel came to Paul at night in the middle of a violent sea storm to tell him that God would save everyone on the ship (Acts 27:22–24). Scripture mentions destroying angels (Acts 12:23), but here we are concerned with the angels who are "ministering spirits sent to serve those who will inherit salvation" (Hebrews 1:14). These angels protect, heal, and relay God's messages to his children, and they usually appear in human form. The ministry of angels was so common in the New Testament times that the author of Hebrews told his readers, "Do not forget to show hospitality to strangers, for by so doing some people have shown hospitality to angels without knowing it" (13:2).

When I was a cessationist, I never heard or read stories about angelic appearances. Yet once I believed in the gifts of the Spirit, I began to hear angel stories, though most of my church remained cessationist.

A stable, young single woman in my church told me she had been driving on the interstate in our city when she became so ill she was afraid she might pass out and lose control of the car. Then she saw a handsome young man dressed in a black leather jacket hitchhiking along the side of the road. She pulled off the road and picked him up. "Please, sir," she said, "I'm so sick. If you could just drive me to the west side of town where my doctor's office is located, I'll make sure you get a ride to anywhere you want to go." The young man agreed and drove her to her doctor's office. He helped her out of the car and into the doctor's office, where a nurse took her immediately into one of the examination rooms. A few minutes later, the woman realized she had forgotten to thank the young man and arrange for him to get another ride. She walked back into the lobby and asked the receptionist where the young man had gone. The receptionist said, "What young man?"

"The young man who practically carried me in here," the woman answered.

"No one carried you in here! You came in here by yourself and put your keys here on the counter." The young woman thought she was truly sick! She imagined the whole thing had been a hallucination.

A year or so later, she was shopping at the NorthPark Mall in Dallas during the Christmas season. It was night, just as the stores were closing. She had parked her car in an underground garage adjacent to one of the stores in the very last space in the far corner. Directly in front of her car and along the passenger side was a cement wall. The space next to the driver's side was empty.

After she finished her shopping, she went back into the garage. There was no one else in it. Then she heard footsteps coming out of the dark behind her, on the right. She glanced in that direction and saw a man walking toward her. She quickened her pace. The man quickened his pace. She ran, and so did her attacker. As she ran, she fumbled in her purse for her keys. When she got to the door of her car, she knew she wouldn't have time to open the door before the man reached her. She turned to face her attacker. As she did, she saw him stop about thirty feet from her with a terrified look in his eyes. Abruptly, he turned around and ran out of the garage. The woman turned back to her car, and there standing between the cement wall and her car was the young man she had picked up a year or so before on the freeway when she was sick. He was dressed in the same black leather jacket, and he smiled at her. She glanced over her shoulder to make sure her attacker had gone, and when she turned back to the young man to thank him, he had vanished. She walked all around the car, searching for him. There was no door in the cement wall. He was not under the car. He had simply vanished. Then she knew. She had been visited by an angel. Once again, he had saved her life.

I said to her, "I've known you for years. Why have you never told me that story?"

"Because," she said, "you would have called me crazy."

She was right. For years, I had been skeptical of all contemporary supernatural experience. And skeptics can always find convincing reasons to disprove stories that are contrary to their experience. Yet once the Scripture convinced me that God had never stopped doing miracles or speaking to his people, I was overwhelmed with credible stories of the miraculous, both in literature and from contemporary reports.

As a Texas boy, I grew up with an appreciation of the legendary football coach Gene Stallings. He had been one of Bear Bryant's junction boys when he was a player at Texas A&M. He went on to be the head coach at A&M and Alabama, an assistant coach with the Dallas Cowboys during the Tom Landry era, and the head coach of the St. Louis/Phoenix Cardinals. But I never knew the most poignant part of his life.

Stallings had two daughters. Then his son Johnny was born. Johnny was born with Down syndrome. One night when Johnny was very small, Coach Stallings heard a noise coming from his son's bedroom.

> I immediately went to check on him. When I opened the door, I discovered not one but two baby boys sitting in Johnny's crib. They were playing a game known only to them and squealing with laughter. The other baby turned toward me, looked into my eyes with a piercing glance, and then suddenly disappeared. To this day I believe with all my heart that God allowed me to see Johnny's guardian angel momentarily in order to encourage me for the years that lay ahead.[3]

Stallings frequently called young couples who had just learned that their child had Down syndrome to tell them that their child had a guardian angel who would always be with the child.

---

3. Larry Calvin, *No Fear! The Calling of Angels* (Fort Worth, TX: Sweet, 1995), 15–16.

Several members of my family have also had encounters with angels. Angels first came to Leesa in her dreams. Our daughter, Alese, could see angels from the time she was eight years old. Our son Scott could also see angels, and he had genuine visionary experiences at an early age. Once I was in our home by myself. I sat on the living room sofa and prayed a fervent prayer for thirty minutes. I wasn't sure if what I was asking God to do was right. I paused the request and said, "Father, should I be asking for this? I have to know. Please show me." Immediately, the front door opened and eleven-year-old Alese walked in. She said, "Dad! There are lights all around you!" Sometimes angels appeared to her as bright lights.

In August 2000, we lived in our dream home high up on the side of a mountain in Whitefish, Montana. Leesa lay on our bed in the afternoon praying for God to change her. Suddenly, an elderly woman dressed in blue stood beside her bed. She placed her hands on Leesa's forehead and pressed three times. Then she laid her hands on Leesa's cheeks and did the same.

Then she said, "If you want to change, now is the time to change." Leesa was overwhelmed by the love and authority she felt from the woman. Then the woman said, "I have to go now." And Leesa watched her float up through the ceiling and out of our house.

When I came home, she told me what had happened. Neither of us knew what it meant.

That fall, we had dinner at the home of our close friends John and Ingrid. Ingrid said, "Jack, I don't understand this, but this week the Lord told me to begin praying about your departure from Whitefish because you are going to leave here in great pain." Even though Ingrid had spoken impressive prophetic words that had come true, I didn't give much thought to this word. I didn't think I would ever leave the paradise of Whitefish.

At the beginning of December 2000, we were in the mountains of Moravian Falls, North Carolina, at a conference. I left our cabin early in the morning, and Leesa slept in. Leesa was awakened by a young woman standing at the foot of the bed massaging her feet through the covers. She was dressed in a beautiful, multicolored robe. Leesa said, "Would you leave a piece of your robe here so I can show Jack?" The angel smiled and disappeared. We understood none of this.

We lost our secondborn son, Scott, to a drugged-out suicide in our home in the dark morning hours of December 27, 2000. He was twenty-two years old. We left Montana three days later and fell into a new world that was darker and more unforgiving than any we had ever known. Leesa sank into an abyss of grief and demonic condemnation. Just about everything that could go wrong went wrong. God did not take away our pain; he came down into it with us and redeemed it little by little.

Years later, I understood the purpose of Leesa's angelic

visits in those months before we lost Scott. The angel pressed her hands on Leesa's forehead to impart protection against the devil's assault on Leesa's mind following Scott's death. Her hands on Leesa's cheeks imparted protection to limit the damage Leesa's tears could do to her. The angel who massaged her feet imparted strength to Leesa to walk through the greatest darkness she would ever know. And the Lord called Ingrid, one of our closest friends, to pray for grace for us to walk through our greatest trial months ahead of that trial. The Lord prayed for Peter before his greatest trial so that Peter's faith would not fail (Luke 22:31–32). When the devil came to sift us, the Lord did the same for us by sending angels and prayers ahead of time so that our faith might not fail.

I have never seen an angel, but the Lord speaks to me frequently through impressions. Almost every day I pray for those impressions. Every time I stand on a stage, I believe that God will give me impressions about individuals sitting in the audience. And he does. But I have never asked God to appear to me or let me see an angel. Somewhere I read, "You do not have because you do not ask God."[4]

---

4. James 4:2.

Chapter 8

The Audible
Voice of God

In the beginning there was no Scripture and no tradition, just God and the two people he created to rule the earth. God appeared to them and spoke to them in an audible voice. But neither the beauty of God nor the power of his voice could keep them from rebelling against their Creator. By Noah's time, the rebellion was so great that the whole human race was close to demon possession, for human wickedness had become so universal that hearts were continually filled with only evil (Genesis 6:5). God spoke to Noah in an audible voice, telling him to build an ark so he could survive the flood that would wipe out the rebellious race.

After the flood, humanity again collectively rebelled against God at the Tower of Babel. God turned from the masses to a man, Abram, to make him into a nation that would bless all the people of the earth. The patriarchs Abraham, Isaac, and Jacob saw God and heard his audible voice.

No one saw God or heard God like Moses: "The LORD would speak to Moses face to face, as one speaks to a friend" (Exodus 33:11). Because Moses was the mediator of God's covenant with Israel, God spoke to him audibly in the hearing of the people to exalt Moses in the eyes of all Israel: "The LORD said to Moses, 'I am going to come to you in a dense cloud, so that the people will hear me speaking with you and will always put their trust in you'" (Exodus 19:9). The Lord spoke in an audible voice to the whole nation in a way that terrified them so that they would always fear God and know that idols were lifeless and worthless (Exodus 20:18–21).

Another reason God spoke to the whole nation audibly was that keeping the Torah was the most difficult task on earth. One principle that seems to govern the way in which the voice speaks to us is this: *the more difficult the task, the greater the power and clarity of the revelation that assigns the task.* The profound way in which Jesus confronted Paul on the Damascus road was at least partly due to the fact that Paul was being called to a life of extravagant suffering far beyond his human capacity to endure. The audible voice helped Paul to be absolutely sure that his suffering was the perfect will of God and that Jesus would give him the power to endure all the pain until that day when the Son of God would place the eternal crown of righteousness on his head (2 Timothy 4:8).

The audible voice was so common in the life of Moses that it might be natural to suppose the audible voice would be common in the ministry of prophets. But this was not to be the case. When Miriam and Aaron challenged the authority of their little brother Moses, God came down in a pillar of cloud and said to them:

> "When there is a prophet among you,
>> I, the LORD, reveal myself to them in visions,
>> I speak to them in dreams.
> But this is not true of my servant Moses;
>> he is faithful in all my house.
> With him I speak face to face,
>> clearly and not in riddles;
>> he sees the form of the LORD.
> Why then were you not afraid
>> to speak against my servant Moses?"
>
> *Numbers 12:6–8*

After Moses, the appearances of God and the audible voice became the rarest way God speaks.

In the New Testament, the audible voice becomes a Person, the Lord Jesus Christ. The Father spoke audibly to his Son at his baptism (Matthew 3:17), at the transfiguration (Matthew 17:5), and just before the crucifixion (John 12:27–33). In all three of these instances, the audible voice came not for the benefit of Jesus but for those with Jesus.

God spoke to Paul on the Damascus road while he was yet an enemy of Christ (Acts 9:1–9). His traveling companions heard the voice but did not understand it (Acts 9:7; 22:9). Ananias heard the voice in a vision telling him to go minister to Paul (Acts 9:10–16). Peter heard the voice in a trance. It prepared him to understand the inclusion of the Gentiles into the church (Acts 10:9–16). John heard the voice when he was in the Spirit on the Lord's Day, and so began the unfolding of the revelation of the last days (Revelation 1:10–11).

In these examples, the audible voice comes at a turning point in the lives of the saints and in the history of the church. The voice comes when the divine ministry about to be performed is extraordinarily difficult to accept or believe, or when the task about to be undertaken is so hard that it will require the clarity and assurance of an audible voice in order to endure and complete the task. Would Ananias have gone to the greatest persecutor of the church to minister to him without the assurance of an audible voice? Perhaps he would have, but the mercy of God didn't require him to do so. Every time God speaks audibly, it is an act of mercy accommodating our weakness.

Luke adds a feature about the audible voice that the other gospel writers leave out. He wrote that when the audible voice came to Jesus at his baptism, Jesus was praying (Luke 3:21). When the voice came at his transfiguration, Jesus also was praying (Luke 9:28–29). When Paul heard the audible voice in the temple during a trance experience (Acts 22:17–21), he was praying, and so was Peter when he heard the voice speak of bringing the Gentiles into the kingdom (Acts 10:9–16). The few people I know who have heard the audible voice of God have been and are committed to lives of prayer.

Just before Jesus' crucifixion, God spoke audibly to his Son in the presence of witnesses. Jesus said in front of a crowd:

> "Now my soul is troubled, and what shall I say? 'Father, save me from this hour'? No, it was for this very reason I came to this hour. Father, glorify your name!"
>
> Then a voice came from heaven, "I have glorified it, and will glorify it again." The crowd that was there and heard it said it had thundered; others said an angel had spoken to him.
>
> Jesus said, "This voice was for your benefit, not mine. Now is the time for judgment on this world; now the prince of this world will be driven out. And I, when I am lifted up from the earth, will draw all people to myself." He said this to show the kind of death he was going to die.
>
> *John 12:27–33*

Jesus prayed, and his Father answered him audibly in public before a crowd. Jesus said the voice was not for his sake but for the benefit of the people there. Remember the principle "the clearer the revelation, the more difficult the task to come"? Jesus was about to die on a cross, a form of capital punishment reserved for the dregs of society.

The Torah stated that anyone who was hung on a tree was under God's curse (Deuteronomy 21:23). The shameful death on the cross would make it difficult to believe that Jesus was the Messiah. People were certain the Son of God could never become a curse. They underestimated the humility of God, so he spoke audibly to his Son so that the crowd might believe in Jesus as the Son of God when everything was about to indicate otherwise.

Even though God spoke in an audible voice, many in the crowd heard no voice at all. They heard only thunder. The key to hearing the voice of God does not lie in the ears or in the intellect, but in the heart.

Although the audible voice is rare, God's faithful are still hearing it. In 1937, Peter Marshall became the pastor of New York Avenue Presbyterian Church, sometimes called "the church of the presidents," in Washington, DC. He served two terms as chaplain of the Senate. People stood outside in the rain for hours to get a seat in his church. Hundreds were turned away every Sunday. When he was a young man, he worked in the English village of Bamburgh, sixteen miles southeast of the border of his native Scotland. He took a shortcut back to Bamburgh one evening:

> The night was inky black, eerie. There was only the
> sound of the wind through the heather-strained moor-
> land, the noisy clamor of wild muir fowl as his footsteps
> disturbed them, the occasional far-off bleating of a sheep.

Suddenly he heard someone call, *"Peter! . . ."* There was great urgency in the voice.

He stopped, "Yes, who is it? What do you want?"

For a second he listened, but there was no response, only the sound of the wind. The moor seemed completely deserted.

Thinking he must have been mistaken, he walked on a few paces.

Then he heard it again, even more urgently:

"Peter! . . ."

He stopped dead still, trying to peer into that impenetrable darkness, but suddenly stumbled and fell to his knees. Putting out his hand to catch himself, he found nothing there. As he cautiously investigated, feeling around in a semicircle, he found himself to be on the very brink of an abandoned stone quarry. Just one step more would have sent him plummeting into space to certain death.[1]

Early in his ministry, Francis Schaeffer faced a minor crisis. He and his young family needed temporary housing during a transition time but had very little money. They needed a "minor miracle" from the Lord. While Francis was praying about this, he said to God, "Where can we live, Lord? Please show us." Immediately, in response to

---

1. Catherine Marshall, *A Man Called Peter: The Story of Peter Marshall* (1951; repr., Grand Rapids: Chosen, 2002), 28–29.

his question, he heard an audible voice. It wasn't a voice inside his mind. It didn't come from another human. He was alone. The voice simply said, "Uncle Harrison's house."

Although the answer was perfectly clear, it made no sense. Uncle Harrison had never given the Schaeffer family anything, and they thought it would be very unlikely he would offer his house for them to live in. Yet the voice that spoke to Francis was so startling and direct he felt he had to obey it. He wrote to his uncle, asking him what he planned to do with his house for the next year. He was astonished when his uncle replied that he planned to live with his brother for the next year and would like to offer his house rent-free to Francis and his family for a year. Francis Schaeffer claims this was the second time God had spoken to him in an audible voice.[2]

Peter Marshall and Francis Schaeffer were heroes of the orthodox faith in the twentieth century. I was a voracious reader of orthodox theology. When I was in college, I read everything that Schaeffer had written. But I never heard stories like this until I was thirty-seven years old and had begun searching for them.

Over the years, I've noticed that people who have heard the audible voice are often reluctant to talk about it. They want to honor the miraculous ministry of the Holy Spirit

---

2. Edith Schaeffer tells this story in *The Tapestry* (Waco, TX: Word, 1981), 384–85. The audible voice assured them that they were in the will of God during a trying time in their lives.

and encourage others to pursue it, but they don't want to use the voice for self-aggrandizement. There are probably many more examples of God speaking in an audible voice to the orthodox than we will ever know about in this life.

The Internal Audible Voice

Jesus promised his disciples that after he ascended to his Father, they would be persecuted by the highest authorities in the land. He told them not to be afraid because the Holy Spirit would speak to them in that internal audible voice and give them the very words they should say (Luke 12:11–12). Just before Jesus went to his cross, he reiterated this promise. He told them the persecution would be worse than they could imagine. Even their loved ones would betray them, even to death. Even then they were not to worry because he would be with them and would give them "words and wisdom that none of your adversaries will be able to resist or contradict" (Luke 21:12–18).

I have come to expect that God will speak to me in the internal audible voice during times of persecution and pain. When I was going through an extended period of pain, I heard Jesus say, "This is my gift to you." There are some things in us that can only be changed by pain. There are depths in Jesus that can only be reached by pain. There are some magnificent rewards he wants to give us that can only be given to those who have endured pain. I have learned to look on all my pain and persecution as an opportunity for promotion in the kingdom of God. Our God is a great Father. No random, useless pain can sneak by him to afflict his children. The only pain he lets come to us is the pain he intends to redeem, if we will let him.

The internal audible voice of God is not limited to times of pain or persecution. The first time I heard the internal audible voice of God, I stood on a stage in front of my church watching a demon manifest in a woman for whom Dr. John White was praying. That demon had been tormenting the woman for many years, but we didn't know that a demon was the architect of her depression and crippling anxiety, and all we had offered the woman was counseling. Dr. White was a professor of psychiatry who had also been a missionary. He had experience with demonized people in his office and on the mission field. He knew the difference between psychiatric disturbance and demonization. He knew you can't "counsel" demons out of people.

While I watched him pray for this woman, I knelt on the stage to pray for her also, and this sentence formed in my mind: "You are a deceiver and a manipulator, and you're just playing at church." In print those words look like an angry, harsh condemnation. But I "heard" no anger in them. What I heard was an invitation to a new way of life and ministry. All I said was, "Yes, Lord." With my simple agreement, the voice of God had launched me into a new world.

Until that day, the only supernatural experience in my life was my conversion. I couldn't have told you anything about the appearances of God, about his audible voice, or about the angels. I believed in all of it, but it was irrelevant to me. Why study what doesn't happen anymore? I thought God only spoke through Scripture. I was a scriptural ace, and Scripture was all I needed in order to follow God closely. But on Saturday afternoon, April 5, 1986, the voice turned me into a little child longing for Jesus to speak to me again.

I had *stood* on that stage for seven years teaching people to follow biblical principles so they could have a better life. I told them to count their day a success if they had prayed and read the Bible in the morning. But the demonized woman I was praying for *had* prayed and read the Bible every day for years. So had the Pharisees. I hurled obligations at my hearers, hoping their obedience would give them a better life. But Jesus hadn't offered us a better life; he had offered us himself. Until I became a friend of Jesus, all I had to give my friends were obligations. I was deceiving them because I had been deceived. Playing at ministry was all I would ever be able to do until I got on my knees and allowed Jesus to show me his ministry.

That day, God created in me a hunger for his voice. I ransacked Scripture, searching for all the ways God spoke to his people, and I begged him daily to speak to me like that. That's when I learned about his appearances, his audible voice, his angels, and more. After that conference with John White, God sent people into my life who had heard his voice in different ways. Then he spoke to me and Leesa in different ways. Leesa had some "spectacular" experiences hearing God, while God spoke to me mostly in impressions. I've said it before, but I'll say it again. I can't repeat it too much. In the beginning, I thought the reason God was speaking to me was to guide me in my service to Jesus. I didn't know then that it gave him pleasure to speak to me and to teach me to love what he loved. He wanted to be friends with me.

Chapter 9

Impressions and Sensations

Outside of Scripture, the most common way the Holy Spirit speaks to me is through impressions. These are thoughts, perceptions, feelings, or understandings that seem to come out of nowhere. They don't have the certainty or the clarity of God's internal audible voice. They come without any rational evidence or logical inference to support their truth. Impressions from the Holy Spirit are *different* from intuition in respect to their origin. A divine impression comes to us from the Holy Spirit, while intuition arises from within our human spirit.

Some people use a technique called "cold reading" to give the appearance they are receiving a supernatural impression about a person. For example, a "prophet" notices pet hair on a woman's dress and says to her, "The Lord shows me that you love animals." Then he may continue to observe her appearance or body language for other clues, phrasing statements in such a way that the woman's response gives him additional information. Professional gamblers are highly skilled at reading signs given by demeanor and body language. They call these signs "tells" because they "tell" them something about the person they are observing.

Impressions from the Holy Spirit are not like cold reading or observing a tell, for they don't come from our observations or logical inferences. Often an impression from the Holy Spirit will communicate knowledge that is the opposite of what our minds think or our senses tell us.

I spoke about the supernatural ministry of the Holy Spirit to six people preparing to be missionaries from a denomination that did not believe in the contemporary miraculous ministry. As I looked at a young guy with the sculpted body of a weight lifter, I had an impression that he had arthritic pain in his neck. *It can't be him*, I thought. I looked at an elderly woman in the group and thought, *It must be her.* I said, "Ma'am, do you have arthritic pain in your neck?"

She said, "No."

The weight lifter said, "I do, and it's severe." Since that experience, I try to discount my opinions and act on the impressions alone.

The Bible has different ways of describing impressions. Nehemiah told how God led him by an impression: "So my *God put it into my heart* to assemble the nobles, the officials and the common people for registration by families" (Nehemiah 7:5, emphasis added). Nehemiah was able to discern that this impression on his heart had come from God, not from himself.

While Paul preached in Lystra, there was a man in the audience who had been lame since birth. Paul "*saw* that he had faith to be healed" (Acts 14:9, emphasis added). Paul commanded the man to stand up, and he was instantly healed. You can't literally *see* faith. In this context, the word *saw* means that Paul had an impression about the man. Impressions may lead to miracles.

Another way of describing an impression may be found in the story of the paralyzed man who was lowered through the roof in front of Jesus. When Jesus told the man his sins were forgiven, "some teachers of the law were sitting there, thinking to themselves, 'Why does this fellow talk like that? He's blaspheming! Who can forgive sins but God alone?'" (Mark 2:6–7). They hadn't said a word out loud, but in their hearts they were furious with Jesus. "Immediately Jesus *knew in his spirit* that this was what they were thinking in their hearts" (Mark 2:8, emphasis added). Often divine impressions are just like that, an immediate knowing in our spirit. It is a form of knowledge that does not come to us through logical reasoning or personal observation. Suddenly we just know that we know.

Sometimes God will give a spiritual impression while we are contemplating something physical. Solomon had a truth about the value of diligence and discipline reinforced when he considered the ways of ants (Proverbs 6:6–8). Paul wrote that God uses the creation to impress us with his greatness (Romans 1:18–20).

I believe God speaks to us through impressions all the time, but many Christians have trained themselves to ignore their impressions. They've been taught that feelings are bad or unreliable. Before I believed in the voice of God, I sometimes found my prayers interrupted by an impression out of nowhere to pray for something I hadn't thought of. I tried to dismiss these pesky interruptions because they weren't on my prayer list. It's as though I said to the Holy Spirit, "Get out of here. I'm trying to pray!" The Holy Spirit tried to lead me to pray for what he wanted to grant, but my theology would not let me listen to him.

The rationalism of Western tradition is offended by knowledge that bypasses the logical workings of the mind. Sometimes God must remove our confidence in our intelligence before he can talk with us.

Impressions often come to me when I teach. In the mid-1990s, I spoke to 1,200 people at a conference in a suburb of Karlsruhe, Germany. I stared at a small section of fifty people on my left. I had an impression that someone in that section was contemplating suicide. I pointed my finger at the section and said, "One of you in this section is thinking of taking your life. Would you come forward so we can pray for you?" A woman in a white dress got up and came forward. I was not even conscious of the fact that when I pointed to the section, I pointed directly at her. Years later, I spoke at a men's conference in upstate New York. The speaker before me revealed that he had planned his own suicide, but the Lord intervened and saved his life. At the conclusion of his message, he said, "I think there is someone here who is thinking of taking his life. Would you come forward so we can pray for you?" No one came forward. I was sure that speaker was right. I walked onto the stage to support him, and "five" popped into my mind. I said, "I think there are five of us here today who are thinking of taking our lives. Don't be embarrassed. God is here to help." Five men came forward. One was a man from my own church. I'd had no idea he was struggling with suicidal thoughts. If we had been content only to teach that day, we might have lost some good men.

At the conclusion of a service, I usually stand at the front of the church with the elders or a prayer team to pray for individuals. When people ask me to pray for them, I silently ask God to show me how to pray before I pray out loud. In 1993, I did series of conferences in the coastal cities of Taiwan. After a service concluded, someone brought to me a twenty-four-year-old woman whose fingers were curled from arthritis. As I took her hands in mine, I prayed silently, "Lord, she's too young for arthritis. What caused this?" Immediately, the words "failed romance, fired" popped into my mind. I put her hands down and asked through an interpreter, "How long have your hands been like this?"

"I'm not sure. Maybe three years, maybe a little longer," she said.

"About four years ago, were you going through any kind of trauma?" I asked.

"No," she said.

"About that time, did you break up with a boy?" I asked.

"Oh, I forgot about that. My boyfriend left me," she said.

"About that same time, did you lose a job?" I asked.

She wept. Her story was that her best friends had been her pastor and his wife. She was the church secretary. They fired her for incompetence, and she regarded it as the greatest betrayal of her life. She said, "They're here at this conference, and it just kills me to look at them."

I told her she had to forgive them. She argued with me for at least ten minutes, claiming that they did not deserve forgiveness. But finally she agreed to forgive them.

"How do I do it?" she asked.

"Ask God to forgive you for holding anger in your heart toward them all these years. Then tell the Lord that you forgive them from your heart," I said.

She wept again as she forgave them. Then I took her gnarled fingers in my hands and asked God to heal her. The five of us on my healing team watched her fingers straighten in seconds. We laughed. We cried. We rejoiced.

That miracle pounded into my heart the necessity of hearing God when I pray for healing. It was also one of the most graphic examples I have seen of someone being tormented in the prison of unforgiveness, a prison that Jesus warned us of (Matthew 18:21–35). Unforgiveness is a major demonic inroad into our lives (2 Corinthians 2:5–11; Ephesians 4:26–27). The master of hate is so skillful at concealing our unforgiveness from us that frequently only the Lord can reveal to us our agreement with the devil and empower us to forgive the one who hurt us.

Forgiving the ones who wounded us does not mean we deny the severity of what they did to us or excuse it in some other way. It means we give up our right to justice and, instead, pray for God to bless them. Some of my wounds have been so severe that it has taken me years to completely forgive my wounders. It helps me to imagine myself standing beside Jesus in heaven, looking down on my wounder. I turn to Jesus and ask him what he wants for my wounder. And before he answers, I know what he wants, and I pray for my wounder to become a close friend of Jesus. I keep doing this until the pain of the wound is wholly healed.[1]

The Lord frequently gives us impressions when we are not praying. We've all had the experience of not being able to shake an impression to call a friend. Finally, we make the call, and it leads to a blessing for one or both of us.

Sometimes God will give us impressions that don't make sense initially. Just after I started to hear the voice of God, I spoke at a conference in San Luis Obispo on the central coast of California. We had all bowed our heads. People in the audience prayed silently for healing. A few of us on the stage asked God to show us how to begin praying for sicknesses and other needs. An unusual disease popped

---

1. For a fuller discussion of what it means to forgive someone, see my book *Why I Am Still Surprised by the Power of the Spirit* (Grand Rapids: Zondervan, 2020), 145–47.

into my mind. I can't remember the disease because of what happened next. I opened my eyes and saw a dime and a penny on top of a guitar monitor. I stared at the dime and penny and felt there was a message in that eleven cents. I asked, "What does the eleven cents mean, Lord?" Then I thought it must mean that eleven people had this disease. So I called out the disease and said, "I think there are eleven people here who have this condition.[2] Would you please come forward so we can pray for you?" There were only five hundred people in the room, and it seemed unlikely that eleven of them had this rare condition. I gave the word anyway because by this time, I had learned that the only way to learn to hear God's voice well was to fail—a lot. I used to say, "You have to be willing to fail." But the truth is that no one becomes great at anything without failing at it a lot in the beginning. That afternoon, eleven people with this disease came forward for prayer. I can't remember if anyone was healed. But I remember what God taught me about his voice. There is no detail too small or unusual that he won't use it to teach us how to hear his voice, even something as random as a dime and a penny lying on a guitar monitor.

I rely on divine impressions for guidance in everyday affairs, as well as for directions in ministry. These impressions have grown more frequent and specific, even to the point of knowing someone's name without ever having

---

2. When I give words to a crowd, I rarely say, "Someone has _____." I usually say, "I think someone here has _____?"

met them or knowing a condition that God wants to heal in a person when no one has told me about that condition. I have observed the same thing happening to many other Christians who:

1. Believe that God will speak to them through impressions.
2. Want these impressions for the joy of hearing God and being better able to serve God and his people.
3. Pray regularly for God to speak to them.
4. Act on the impressions when they come, even at the risk of looking foolish in front of others.

Sensations

One day when Jesus was being mobbed by a crowd, a woman who had been bleeding for twelve years sneaked up behind him and touched the edge of his cloak. She was healed immediately. Jesus asked, "Who touched me?" Peter answered by pointing out that everyone was touching the Lord and that his question made no sense. Jesus said, "Someone touched me; *I know that power has gone out from me.*" The healed woman confessed, and Jesus said to her, "Daughter, your faith has healed you. Go in peace" (Luke 8:43–48, emphasis added). Jesus was so kind to the woman. He wanted her to know that there was no magic in his cloak. The healing power was in *him*, and it was her faith that released his power, so that even when he was gone from her, she would still have access to his healing mercy.

Just as the Father spoke to his Son through a physical sensation in the body of Jesus, God will sometimes speak to us through physical sensations in our body. When I stand onstage asking God to show me whom or what he wants to heal, sometimes I will feel a pressure or a pulsing on my body. It's not painful. It's a sign. It usually means that God wants to heal someone in the room in that part of their body.

This shouldn't surprise us. We are more than minds. Why wouldn't God speak to us in our bodies? He gives us pain in our bodies to warn us. Why wouldn't he use physical sensations in our bodies to guide us in healing others? I know something like this happens in New Age groups. But New Age groups also pray and fast. Should we give up prayer and fasting? Satan is a counterfeiter. He began his earthly counterfeiting in the Garden of Eden. The devil raised up religious unbelievers to attribute the work of Jesus to evil powers. The theologians of the first century thought Jesus broke the food laws and the Sabbath laws, but he actually fulfilled those laws. Sometimes Jesus comes to us in ways that make it easy for us to reject him. When he does that, he is teaching us not to rely solely on our own discernment, on our own interpretation of Scripture, but to come to him for revelation.

Every time I teach a group of people how God speaks, I lead them in a practice time. I invite them to bow their heads and ask God to show them someone or something he wants to heal or someone he wants to give a prophetic message to. I tell them to wait for an impression, a picture, or a sensation in their bodies. I wait for a few minutes in silence. Then I say, "I want to begin with someone who thinks God may have spoken to them, but you have never raised your hand in a public meeting to give a healing or a prophetic word."

At least 90 percent of the time, that first-timer is right. I am showing people how easy it is to hear God's voice when we want to minister to his people. During these practice times, when someone has a physical sensation, like warmth in their right ear, I ask if anyone sitting close to the person with the physical sensation has anything wrong with their right ear. Almost always it is someone sitting close by, just like the woman with the hemorrhage was close to Jesus. I tell them that if this happens to them on a Sunday morning in church, they should look around them and ask God to show them the person who needs healing in that part of their body. If God shows them a person, I encourage them to ask if they can pray for them.

When I was a professor and a pastor, I had turned my church into a lecture hall. No one but me used their spiritual gift on Sundays. I thought my main job was to teach Scripture. I put in twenty years of ministry before I saw that the leaders of the first-century Christians taught their followers to use their gifts so they can do the work of the ministry (Ephesians 4:11–13).

The first Christians not only gathered to hear a speaker and to worship, but they also came to pray (Acts 2:42) and to give away gifts. Paul told the Corinthians that they could bring a hymn, a teaching, a revelation, a tongue, or an interpretation to give away when they came to church (1 Corinthians 14:26).[3] His list was not exhaustive, but it simply illustrated the kinds of gifts Christians were to bring to the worship services.

I go to all kinds of churches all over the world today. The fastest-growing and most-powerful churches are the churches where many people in the church are using their spiritual gifts to be a blessing to others.

---

3. The Corinthians were abusing spiritual gifts, especially the gift of tongues. We might expect Paul to quell their enthusiasm for the spiritual gifts, but he didn't. He corrected the abuse and told them to pursue spiritual gifts diligently and use them with love, especially prophecy (1 Corinthians 14:1). There are twenty-one spiritual gifts. God gave them to be used, not simply to be studied.

Chapter 10

Dreams and Visions

Dreams. Never had much use for them when I was a Bible deist. I knew that God had used them at one time, but we weren't that hard up anymore now that we had the completed Scriptures. The Bible rendered that whole dangerous, shadowy, visionary world irrelevant. When the apostle John finally went up to heaven, God slammed the door shut on the whole supernatural world down here. I lived in the safe world of teachers, seminary professors, and elders—the well-off, successful businessmen who made policy for the church I led. I was married to the most beautiful girl I had ever seen. We had three great kids. I had it made.

A graduate of a Baptist seminary came to our church and dated one of our single women we had known for a long time. He was a nice guy. Then they got engaged. Just before the wedding, my beautiful bride came to breakfast and told me a weird dream she had the night before: the seminary boy abused our church girl. Leesa said, "And it was bad. What do you think that means?" she asked.

"It can't be true. He's a good guy. Must have been a nightmare," I said. But Leesa never had nightmares. One of our pastors married the couple. They divorced not too long afterward. She couldn't endure his abuse. We never saw him again.

A thoughtful pastor might have given a little thought to studying dreams after that episode. But it would be years before I was provoked into studying the voice and saw the prominence of dreams and visions in the world of the Holy Spirit.

God's classic word on dreams is Job 33:13–18.

> Why do you complain to him
> > that he responds to no one's words?
> For God does speak—now one way,
> > now another—
> > though no one perceives it.
> In a dream, in a vision of the night,
> > when deep sleep falls on people
> > as they slumber in their beds,
> he may speak in their ears
> > and terrify them with warnings,
> to turn them from wrongdoing
> > and keep them from pride,
> to preserve them from the pit,
> > their lives from perishing by the sword.

The first dream in the Bible is the warning dream that God gave to the Philistine king Abimelek in Genesis 20:3, and it did terrify the Philistine. Joseph and Daniel were major dreamers. Dreams and visions are the normal language God uses to speak to his prophetic people (Numbers 12:6–8). Dreams were prominent during the birth of Jesus. When the Holy Spirit came on the Day of Pentecost to live in the people of God, Peter promised them that young and old, boys and girls, would dream dreams and see visions (Acts 2:17–18).[1] And that prophecy came without any shelf life. It was meant for the life of the church. The last book of the Bible is an extended vision.

The Purposes of Dreams

Warnings

Why use a dream instead of the clarity of a printed verse? Some dreams can be terrifying. The terror can be more effective at changing our behavior than a prosaic warning. After some of his dreams, Daniel was so shaken that all his strength left him and he became ill.[2] When we sleep, our emotions are vulnerable because our rational guard is down. While awake, a person may be able to justify committing a certain sin, but in a dream, that person feels the pain of

---

1. These verses do not mean that all Christians are prophets, but all Christians can prophesy, just as all Christians are not evangelists, but all Christians can evangelize. God speaks to all kinds of people in dreams, although he speaks in dreams most frequently to prophets. That is why prophets tend to be the most gifted people in interpreting dreams.

2. Daniel 7:28; 8:27; 10:8–17.

irreversible damage and of consequences he never imagined from that sin, and then they wake up so glad to find out it was a dream, and they have a new resolve to trust God.

Dreams can overcome our prejudices and other defenses in a way arguments can't. We can stop listening to or reading thoughts we disagree with, but we can't turn off a dream until it finishes.

My secondborn son, Scott, struggled with drug addiction from the time he was thirteen. He spent seven months in one rehab. But he always went back to drugs. When he was twenty, he called me one morning and told me that in his dream during the night, he died from an overdose and lay dead, curled in the fetal position. When he awoke, he was curled in the same fetal position as in the dream. He was terrified.

"Dad, what does that mean?" he asked.

"Scott, it means you are going to die if you don't stop doing drugs," I said.

"I'm going to stop, Dad," he said.

"I know you will, Scott," I said.

I prayed for Scott more than I prayed for anybody. I believed he had a divine calling on his life like mine. I believed Scott would stop doing drugs and join me on the stage where I ministered. I believed that with all my heart until the morning I found him dead on his bedroom floor. Scott was one month shy of his twenty-third birthday. Even though God will use dreams to terrify us, he won't bulldoze the dignity of our free choice with dreams.

Revealing How God Feels

Sometimes a dream that terrifies us was meant to encourage us. A young woman came to me scared to death that God had told her she was going to be raped. In the dream, some men had tied her hands behind her back and strangled her with a string of her pearls while they raped her. She and her husband were pastors on the staff of a large church, and the pastors were in a conflict. I took the dream to a prophetic person. He said the "rape" represented what some of the pastors were doing to this couple. They were trying to take away the reputation of this couple and the ministry that God had given them in the church. The hands tied behind her back meant they were making their accusations behind the couple's back so that they had no way to defend themselves. The string of pearls meant the pastors were torturing her with her most precious "possession"—her husband. Their attack on her husband was choking the life out of her. Then the prophet said, "Jack, tell her God gave her this dream to show her how he feels about what is being done to her and her husband. It is a rape in his eyes. If they can keep their hearts clean and respond openly and calmly to the accusations, God will vindicate them."

The dream was such an encouragement to the couple that they were able to rise above the hatred of the schemers and not retaliate. In the end, the couple was vindicated.

Guidance

On Paul's second missionary journey, God gave him a vision in the night "of a man of Macedonia standing and begging him, 'Come over to Macedonia and help us'" (Acts 16:9). On this occasion, a dream or night vision was God's means of guiding Paul to the place where the Lord wanted him to minister. I've already mentioned that this was one of the verses that caused me to see that we needed more than our knowledge of the Bible to help us fulfill God's highest purposes for our lives. I hadn't yet studied dreams in the Bible, so I didn't know how extensively God used dreams to communicate to his followers and even to his enemies. And I had no idea I was married to a major dreamer.

Shortly after we had come to believe in the supernatural ministry of the Holy Spirit, we were at a party with some of our new prophetic friends. John Paul Jackson said to Leesa, "You have a prophetic gift. God is going to give you prophetic dreams soon." Starting that night, Leesa had a horrible nightmare almost every night. In one nightmare, someone was shooting her with a machine gun. She tried to fall down so she could die, but the stream of bullets kept her propped up so she could be shot over and over. I called John Paul and said, "What did you do to my wife? Ever since your prophecy, she has had severe nightmares."

"Oh," he said, "I forgot to tell you about that. Sometimes when God begins to give a person prophetic dreams, the process starts with nightmares. I think God may be cleaning out the system to prepare the way for purer dreams. Just lay your hands on Leesa at bedtime and ask God to protect her sleep, and she'll be fine." I did what he said, and it worked—no more nightmares.

After Leesa's dreams began, I was about to make a commitment to help someone build a ministry to churches. I liked him immensely. So did Leesa. This person praised me and celebrated my gifts. Then Leesa saw him in a dream in which he was a guest on the Johnny Carson show. Carson was a famous late-night talk show host back then. Our new friend was doing elaborate backflips and landing on women seated in chairs on the stage. He was laughing and oblivious to the pain he caused the women. The audience applauded and yelled as he did the somersaults. In the dream, Leesa felt horrible about the damage he inflicted on the women. At breakfast she said, "I think the women represented churches. It is not in his heart to serve the churches. He wants to use them to become famous, and he will hurt the churches in the process." I couldn't come up with a better interpretation than Leesa's, but I still wanted to make the commitment to him.

I decided to ignore the dream and commit to helping him. As I walked into a pharmacy, I was still arguing with God. In my silent prayer, I said, "Lord, I just can't see these ugly tendencies in my friend." Then the internal audible voice said, "Why do you think I gave you the dream?" I didn't make the commitment, and subsequent history verified the truth of Leesa's dream. I was so glad not to be joined to him. This was the first of many times that Leesa's dreams saved us or guided us.

Commands

In a dream, God said to Jacob, "Now leave this land at once and go back to your native land" (Genesis 31:13). When Laban wanted to harm Jacob, God came to Laban in a dream and said, "Be careful not to say anything to Jacob, either good or bad" (31:24). I've already mentioned the prominence of dreams at the birth of Jesus. Gabriel came to both Zechariah and Mary, telling them what to name their sons (Luke 1:13, 31). God sent an angel in a dream to command Joseph to take Mary as his wife and to name her son Jesus (Matthew 1:20–21). The angel came in another of Joseph's dreams telling him to take Jesus and Mary to Egypt (2:13). After Herod died, another angel came to Joseph in a dream telling him to leave Egypt and take Mary and the baby Jesus back to Israel (2:19–20). The Lord gave him another dream telling him to take his family out of Judea to Galilee (2:22). The Lord also commanded the Magi in a dream not to go back to Herod (2:12).

Encouragement

When Paul first came to Corinth, he went to the synagogue every Sabbath, preaching the gospel. Eventually he was forced to leave the synagogue. Paul's Jewish enemies had hounded him in almost every city he had visited.

Once before, some of the Jews from Antioch had come to Lystra and managed to get a crowd so worked up that they stoned Paul and left him for dead. Now the same process was starting at Corinth. Some key synagogue leaders had become believers in Christ, and Paul knew it wouldn't take too long for his enemies to retaliate. Would he be stoned again?

It was in this context that "one night the Lord spoke to Paul in a vision: 'Do not be afraid; keep on speaking, do not be silent. For I am with you, and no one is going to attack and harm you, because I have many people in this city'" (Acts 18:9–10). This vision brought great comfort and encouragement to Paul. I'm sure Paul would have stayed in the city until God told him to leave, even if it meant he would be stoned again. But how kind it was of the Lord to take those worries out of Paul's mind by giving him this vision. I find it is common for the Lord to give comfort and encouragement through dreams and visions.

Revealing the Future

God can use dreams to reveal the immediate future or even the events of the last days. When Joseph was a young man, he was given two dreams about the immediate future that indicated that one day he would be elevated to a position of leadership (Genesis 37:5–11). Both Daniel and John were given dreams and visions that not only related to the course of world history in their time but also stretched down into the events of the last days.

Dreams can warn us of events that are decreed by God, that is, events that are surely going to happen. Pharaoh had the same dream in two different forms. First, he saw seven fat cattle being eaten by seven skinny cattle, and then seven fat heads of grain being eaten by seven skinny heads of grain. Joseph said to Pharaoh, "The reason the dream was given to Pharaoh in two forms is that the matter has been firmly decided by God, and God will do it soon" (Genesis 41:32). The dream meant that after seven prosperous years, a seven-year famine was coming. It would have been useless to ask God to withhold the famine. He had already decreed it. The dream was meant as a warning so that the people could prepare for the famine ahead of time.[3]

Other dreams warn us of *potential* events that can be averted by our prayers or our repentance. Nebuchadnezzar had a dream about a man whose mind was changed into that of an animal (Daniel 4:16). Daniel told Nebuchadnezzar that the dream referred to the king himself. The disaster could have been averted, for Daniel said to Nebuchadnezzar, "Renounce your sins by doing what is right, and your wickedness by being kind to the oppressed. It may be that then your prosperity will continue" (v. 27). God gave Nebuchadnezzar one year in which to repent of his pride and arrogance, but

---

3. Other dreams that occurred in two different forms and represented decreed events are found in Genesis 37:5–11. The dreams in Daniel 2 and 7 represented the progress of world empires beginning with the Babylonian kingdom.

when Nebuchadnezzar failed to repent, God brought on him the disaster warned about in the dream (vv. 28–33).

It has been my experience that most of the negative dreams we have are those that warn us of sins or calamities that can be averted by prayer or repentance. If we are uncertain whether the dream is a warning or a decreed event, we can pray for the interpretation and God will give us understanding, for he gave us the dream to guide us. He wants us to understand his voice.

Appearances of the Lord

When the Lord appears to someone in Scripture, there is a level of intimacy and communion with God that transcends other less personal dreams and visions. A great example is when the Lord appeared to Solomon at Gibeon and carried on an extended conversation with him (1 Kings 3:5–15).

The second time the Lord appeared to Leesa was in a dream. She was overcome by his beauty and compassion. She said, "If I could look into his face for all eternity, I would be perfectly happy. I wouldn't want anything else. It was that wonderful. Whenever I feel guilty about something, I think about Jesus' face, and the guilt lifts." Other friends to whom the Lord has appeared have said the same thing to me.

It is not uncommon for a "faceless" man to appear to believers in a dream. I believe the faceless man represents the Holy Spirit, whose primary task is to point us to the face of Jesus Christ.

Speaking to Unbelievers

Some Christians claim that God does not speak to unbelievers, but the Bible shows that he does. In the Old Testament, he spoke to unbelievers through the prophets, but he also spoke to them in more direct ways. It wasn't at all uncommon for God to speak to rulers through dreams. He spoke this way to Abimelek (Genesis 20:3–7), to Pharaoh (41:1–7), and to Nebuchadnezzar (Daniel 2:1–45; 4:9–18). He also spoke in dreams to those who weren't rulers (for example, the Midianite soldier in Judges 7:13). In the New Testament, God spoke to Pilate's wife in a dream, but when she told her husband the dream, he ignored her warning (Matthew 27:19). God also spoke to the Magi, who were probably pagan astrologers, in a dream, warning them not to return to Herod (Matthew 2:12).

God still speaks to unbelievers in dreams, and there is a growing interest in dreams outside the church. When we listen sympathetically to the dreams of our unbelieving friends, we may find that Jesus is opening a door in their hearts, even if he had not sent the dream.

Is the Dream from God?

The more we try to listen to God, the more we pray to hear his voice, the more we risk looking foolish, the more we fail, the better we will get at hearing his voice. This is true with impressions, and it is true with dreams. It is rare for anyone to learn to hear the voice of the Lord all by themselves. We need to be part of a community of believers who are seeking to hear the voice of the Lord. And we need mentors to help us. John Wimber was a great mentor for me in healing and in hearing God. John Paul Jackson and Mike Bickle were an incredible help in understanding prophetic ministry. John Paul was the best I've ever seen at interpreting dreams and a great help to me in learning how to interpret dreams.

I dream every night, but most of my dreams are not from the Lord. Dreams from the Lord tell a coherent and meaningful story. They frequently terrify us or give us hope or surprise us. They seem important and usually reflect a viewpoint different from the dreamer's.

If I'm still uncertain whether the dream is from the Lord, I ask him to speak to me about the dream. If the dream is from him, he will eventually confirm it if I continue to pray about the dream. The ambiguity of the origin of the dream is all part of the process of leading us to depend on God so that our friendship with him is deepened. The ultimate purpose of everything that happens to us is to draw us closer to God.

Interpreting Dreams and Visions

Dreams are fleeting and easily forgotten (Job 20:8). When I think the dream is from the Lord, I record it. If I don't write the dream down within five minutes of waking up, I will probably forget it. That's why Daniel "wrote down the substance of his dream" (Daniel 7:1). I have woken up in the middle of the night with the most powerful dream and thought I would never forget it. I went back to sleep, and the next morning all I could remember was that I'd had a powerful dream during the night. I keep my phone beside the bed so I can record a dream immediately on waking. I have a computer file for each calendar year, and I write the exact date of the dream at the top of the page. I also keep a file folder for each member of my family, as well as files for some of our prophetic friends. This way I can review the dreams. It can be a year or more before we understand the meanings of dreams that turn out to be important for us.

One of the common interpretive mistakes is to take dreams too literally. Consider Leesa's Johnny Carson dream. Every element was symbolic except for the main actor. Symbols often make our dreams difficult to interpret. But the blessing of symbols is that they cause us to depend on God to understand our dreams. Both Joseph and Daniel were emphatic that the interpretation of dreams belongs to God.[4] Another blessing of dreaming in symbols we don't normally use and can't easily understand is that this is a sign the dream is not coming out of some conscious opinion we hold.

Another common mistake is wrongly interpreting the

---

4. Genesis 40:8; 41:16, 25, 28, 39; Daniel 1:17; 2:28; 4:18.

timing of a prophetic dream. One reason for writing down dreams and prophetic words is that it may be years before they come to pass. Joseph's dreams of his family bowing down to him took twenty years to fulfill.[5] Joseph probably drew hope from those dreams while he was in prison. Usually, the greater the blessing promised in the dream, the longer it takes to come to pass. Those dreams of future blessing are meant to sustain us during hard times. Often there will be a key feature of the dream I can't interpret. My part is to pray for the interpretation and to believe God will give it to me, as well as the right application, in time for me to benefit from the dream.

Some symbols are common in dreams. Flowing water often represents the Holy Spirit. Flowing fresh water, like springs, often represents a fresh work of the Holy Spirit. Trains sometimes represent movements, like the Vineyard movement. Cars frequently represent a particular ministry. I've already mentioned that a faceless man in a dream may be the Holy Spirit. Airplanes show that someone or something is moving in a high realm (for example, finances or influence or godliness or something else important to the dreamer). Colors often have significance. Blue frequently refers to revelation or heaven. Black can be evil or sin. Purple is royalty. Symbols can also reveal the perspective of God. When Nebuchadnezzar dreamed about four

---

5. Joseph was seventeen when he had the dreams (Genesis 37:2) and thirty-seven when the brothers came to Egypt (41:46, 53–54).

successive world empires, he saw them as a "dazzling statue" (Daniel 2:31). But when Daniel dreamed about them, he saw them as four wild beasts (7:3–7).

Often it is helpful to make a list of the commonplace associations of a symbol in the dream. If a "fox" is a prominent symbol in the dream, the clue to its meaning may be a commonplace association of foxes. What do people commonly associate with foxes? Look first in Scripture, where people think of foxes as "destructive" (Song of Songs 2:15) or "sly" (Luke 13:32). I look for commonplaces in the Bible, in my own experience, and then in the world at large.

Any detail that stands out in a dream is important for the interpretation of the dream. In one of my dreams, I noticed how straight and perfectly spaced the white lines in a parking lot were. The dream was about a movement, and I took the perfect white lines to mean that the individual ministries in that movement were rigidly controlled. I also try to remember my feelings in the dream because they can be a clue to the meaning of the dream.

Anyone who dreams regularly will acquire a personal set of symbols. When John Wimber's wife, Carol, had a dream with her youngest grandson in it, he always represented the Vineyard Church of Anaheim. That church was John and Carol's "baby."

Dreams and visions are the normal language of prophets. So it makes sense that prophets are the best at interpreting dreams.

Misuse of Dreams

Dreams are not given to enhance our stature in the church or give us control over others. Some things the Lord shares with us are meant to be kept to ourselves. I believe the Lord wants a secret history with each of his children. I value transparency and vulnerability. But there are some things we are to share only with the Lord. Jesus made a great promise to those who overcome and continue in a deep friendship with him: "To the one who is victorious, I will give some of the hidden manna. I will also give that person a white stone with a new name written on it, known only to the one who receives it" (Revelation 2:17).

Sometimes dreams are meant to teach us how to pray about a situation or how to pray for certain people. The fact that we have had a dream doesn't mean we have permission to share it with others, even though they may have appeared in the dream. God may give us a dream that indicates he is going to do something wonderful for us. This makes us feel special, and we may want to tell other people about the dream so that they can see how special we are to God. He may have given us the dream because we are about to go through an excruciatingly difficult time and will need all the encouragement we can get from him to make it through. By telling the dream to others, we may be giving in to pride and increasing the difficulty of the trial.

This is what happened to Joseph. He had two dreams

indicating that God was going to promote him to a high level of leadership. Then he unwisely told the dream to his brothers, who already hated him because of the favoritism shown to him by their father (Genesis 37:5). Instead of working in Joseph's favor, the telling of the dream increased the pain in his life. God worked it all out in the end for everyone's benefit, but Joseph was still unwise to tell the dream.

Visions

Visions are like dreams, except the visionary is awake, at least when the vision begins. The vision could be a single picture or a major story, like the apostle John's vision in the book of Revelation. John Wimber used to get pictures all the time. While walking through an airport, he saw a dark spot on a man's back. The man was standing outside a bookstore. "Excuse me, sir. Do you have pain in your back?" asked John.

"Yes," the man answered.

"Is it right here?" John asked as he put his finger into the center of the dark spot.

"Ow! That's it," he said.

"I see the Lord heal people all the time. Could I pray for you?" asked John.

"Here?" asked the man.

"Well," said John, "we could go into the men's room, but I think here would be better."

The man was probably healed, but I don't remember that part of the story. John was always seeing things about people in airports and on airplanes.

Once I started praying for people as a way of life, it became normal for me to see visions. In the mid-1990s, I spoke at the Church of St. John the Divine in Houston, Texas. At the time, it was one of the largest Episcopal churches in the country. My message focused on hearing the voice of God, and at one point I said, "Sometimes the Lord will show you a picture." While I was speaking that sentence, I saw an esophagus dangling from the ceiling on my right. I kept talking, but I didn't take my eyes off the esophagus. It danced all the way across the room. When it hit the left side, it disappeared. I wondered why it had danced across the room. I stopped the message and said, "I think there are a number of people here who have esopha-geal problems. If you have reflux esophagitis, hiatal hernias, or anything else wrong with your esophagus, would you please stand so we can pray for you." It seemed like a quarter of the room stood. For weeks, I received reports of people healed of esophageal issues. Later, I understood why the esophagus had danced across the room that day. The Lord was telling me that people all over the room were suffering from esophagus pain.

In the New Testament, most sickness appeared to have

natural causes, but some illnesses or dysfunctions are caused by evil spirits. The demons haven't gone anywhere. They still look for open doors to harm people. It is common for healers to see demons oppressing people even before the sick person asks for prayer. The following is a typical story.

In October 2021, Michael Rowntree, Michael Miller, and I were leading a conference at WoodsEdge Church, a large church in the Houston area pastored by Jeff Wells. A young man named Shane from Michael Rowntree's church in Fort Worth came to the conference and listened to me give a message on feeling the affection of God. It became clear to him that he had never felt God's affection. For the first time, he admitted to himself that his whole Christian experience was drudgery, a battle of willpower, and nothing more. Then he went to Michael Miller's breakout session called "Strongholds of the Mind." After the class ended, a woman he had never met said to him, "I felt like the Lord is showing me something about you. Would you mind if I share it?"

During the session, she saw a demonic spirit on Shane. It was like an octopus, having eight arms. Each arm had a label in the vision, and each label began with the prefix *dis*: DISappointment, DISsatisfaction, DISillusionment, and so forth. She thought the Lord wanted to set him free, and she asked if that resonated with him. He said yes. Then she commanded the demon to leave. Shane felt an evil presence rise through his back, sit for a moment over his right shoulder, and then shoot out of his body. For the rest of the conference, and for the first time in his life, he was able to feel the affection of Jesus for him.

Michael Rowntree spoke with him six weeks later, and Shane said his life was completely different. Shane's wife told Michael, "My husband is a different person—night and day. It's a 180-degree change." Now Shane is full of joy. He feels God's affection every time he worships. Worship is no longer drudgery, but a celebration.

Sometimes Christians freak out at the mention of demons, but they shouldn't. Jesus and his apostles regularly drove out demons and never showed the slightest fear. We are the ones with the power, not the demons.[6]

Trances

A trance is a visionary state where it feels like you're being taken out of your body. You have no awareness of your immediate environment. God may use a trance to overcome a natural resistance to something he wants you to do or to show you. The Old Testament does not use the word *trance*, but this seems to best describe what happened to Saul (1 Samuel 19:23–24) and to Daniel (Daniel 10:7–9).

---

6. I write about how demons gain access to people and how to get rid of them in *Why I Am Still Surprised by the Power of the Spirit* (Grand Rapids: Zondervan, 2020), 132–59.

Two additional trances are mentioned in the New Testament. Peter was praying on the roof of the house where he was staying in Joppa when he "fell into a trance." While in the trance, he saw a vision of unclean animals. "Then a voice told him, 'Get up, Peter. Kill and eat.'" But he refused to eat anything unclean. "The voice spoke to him a second time, 'Do not call anything impure that God has made clean.'" This happened three times (Acts 10:9–16). The trance Peter experienced was necessary to break the power of the lie that the Gentiles were too unclean, too impure, to be brought into the body of Christ.

The other trance recorded in the New Testament happened to Paul shortly after Jesus appeared to him on the Damascus road. Paul returned to Jerusalem and was praying in the temple when he fell into a trance. The Lord appeared to him and told him he had to leave Jerusalem because his life was in danger. Paul argued with the Lord until Jesus told Paul he was sending him to the Gentiles (Acts 22:17–21).

God used a trance to overcome Peter's reluctance to accept the Gentiles into the family of God, and Paul's reluctance to leave Jerusalem.

I had been pleading with God to speak to me about people he wanted to be healed, but he hadn't paid any attention to my pleas. For almost a year, every time I tried to give a revelation in public about something or someone God wanted to heal, it was wrong. A student came into my office one afternoon to ask me to accept a late assignment. While he droned on about the assignment, I fell into a trance. Without any warning, I was taken into a vacuum where I could not see or feel my body or see or hear the student. Then out of that nothingness, I saw the word **PORNOGRAPHY**, just like that, in black, bold, capital letters. I came back into my office, and the student was still there talking. When he paused, I asked him if he struggled with pornography. He did, and I offered help with his addiction, promising never to reveal his name. Pornography was only the tip of the iceberg, but the Lord set him free that day. He was a good kid who had fallen into a sexual addiction in his early teen years before he became a believer. He couldn't talk to anyone about his sin because the kind of church he had belonged to exiled those who confessed to sexual sins. He never would have confessed his sin if the Lord had not revealed it.

The second trance I experienced happened a couple of years after I left the seminary. I was in a conference in the middle of a noisy crowd. One second, I was laughing at a joke someone was telling, and in the next instant, I was in that realm of nothingness and total silence again. In that realm, I thought of a miracle I wanted to happen. Then I "heard" a voice say, "If you pray for that miracle, it will happen." When I came back to the crowd, they were still laughing at the same joke. It was as though no time had passed. Later, I prayed for the miracle, and it happened.

A Life-Saving Dream

In February 1988, the children were asleep while Leesa and I read in our family room. "I've been afraid to tell you this," she said, "because I didn't want to worry you unnecessarily. For the last six months, I think God has been telling me that Alese is going to die." I was stunned. Why would God take our seven-year-old daughter? By this time, I had developed profound respect for my wife's ability to hear the voice of the Lord. This time, however, I wanted to believe she was wrong. Would the Lord tell someone ahead of time that their loved one was about to die prematurely, or was this some sort of demonic deception sent to worry us?[7] How were we to decide?

For the last year, Leesa had been having specific and accurate prophetic dreams about people and events. We decided to pray that night and ask God to give her a dream that would tell us if Alese was in any real danger. When I prayed for the dream, I asked the Lord to protect Leesa from any demonic deception or from any influence that might arise out of her own emotions and fears. When she woke up the next morning, Leesa related to me the dream she'd had during the night.

---

7. Yes, the Lord would tell of an impending death. He told Ezekiel he was going "to take away the delight of your eyes." The next day, Ezekiel's wife died (Ezekiel 24:15–27). I knew this passage, but I was so stunned by my wife's message that my mind shut down and I went into panic mode.

In the dream, Leesa found herself lying in the middle of a huge athletic stadium filled with thousands of people. She was lying in the center of the field with a long spear thrust through her heart. People were filing by, looking at her, amazed that she was still alive. As she looked up to the end of the spear, she saw a cross on it. Both of us were convinced that the dream meant that just as Mary's heart was pierced with a sword through her Son's death on the cross, so God was going to take our little Alese from us.

At once I walked into my closet and shut the door and got on my knees. I began to cry and plead with God not to take our youngest child. Then I became angry with the Lord, asking him why he would treat me this way. In the midst of my anger, I remembered that he had also lost a child, but it didn't make any difference to me. Somehow the comparison didn't seem fair. He got his Son back after three days through the resurrection. If he took Alese, how long would it be before I would see her again?

I don't know how long I went on like this, but I know when I came out, my eyes were swollen and I was in despair. I decided to fast and ask God to change his mind. Shortly after the dream, John Paul and his wife, Diane, came to our church. He prayed over our two boys, Stephen and Scott, and said some wonderful things about them. Then he and his wife sat down in front of Alese and started to prophesy over her. He began to say, "The Lord is going to—" but stopped in mid-sentence and said, "We need to pray for the safety of your daughter." Later, he took me aside and said that the devil wanted to kill her. The *devil* wanted to kill her? All this time we had been thinking that the *Lord* was going to take her from us. When we told John Paul about the dream, he said that the dream was a warning dream and that we should pray for Alese every day by laying hands on her and asking the Lord to protect her.

We gathered the children together and told them the devil wanted to attack us. This meant we would need to be more careful than we usually were about where we went and with whom we talked. We let them know we were going to be a little more restrictive with their privileges than was our normal custom. We assured them we would make it through this time just fine if we were careful and prayed every day for God's protection. Every morning, we laid hands on our daughter Alese and asked God to protect her, to surround her with the power of the Holy Spirit, and to send angels with her wherever she went. We did the same thing each night before we went to bed.

One Sunday, shortly after we had begun to do this, I had just finished preaching a sermon at our church. Our friends Doc and Nancy Fletcher had brought Doc's mother, Joy Fletcher, to our church that day. Joy was a Southern Baptist who lived in West Texas and was visiting our church for the first time. After the service, she came up to shake my hand. After shaking hands, I attempted to withdraw my hand, but she held on to it firmly. We were just exchanging small talk, so I couldn't figure out why she wouldn't let go of my hand. After what seemed like a long time, I finally managed to get my hand back and swiftly put it into my pocket. Joy left with Doc, and I talked to other people.

Thirty-five minutes later, when everyone had left the church, Doc and his mother came back. Doc's eyes were red. He had been crying. His mother was somber. He said to me, "Sometimes my mother has visions of people. These visions almost always come true. Four times she has seen a person's death ahead of time. Each time the vision of death has come true. The first time it happened to us was when she saw the death of my nine-year-old brother two weeks before he died. Mom, tell him what you saw."

Joy looked at me and said, "Sometimes when I touch people, I see visions about them. While I was shaking your hand, I saw a brick home that had a driveway running down the side and turning behind the house. Along the driveway was a white iron fence. Then I saw a little girl with long, light brown hair who looked to be about seven or eight years old. She was in the driveway playing when a man walked up to her and—" Her voice trailed off. Joy had accurately described our driveway and our daughter Alese.

"Did the man come to hurt her?" I asked.

"Yes."

"Was he going to kill her?"

"I think that was his plan."

I thanked them for coming back and telling us the

vision. Now we had three independent confirmations that the devil intended to kill our daughter, Alese—my wife's dream, John Paul's impression, and Joy's vision. Out of the mouth of two or three witnesses an event is confirmed. We knew for sure that God was warning us so that our daughter might be spared. We not only continued praying for her, but we also informed the whole church of the satanic attack on our daughter's life and how we had learned about it. We asked our church to pray for us each day until the attack had lifted. Sometime after Easter that spring, we felt like our daughter was out of danger. The attack was over. To this day, my wife and I are convinced that Alese was spared through the warning dream so graciously given to us by our heavenly Father.

Chapter 11

Recognizing the Voice

Four voices regularly speak to us. First, God speaks to us. Second, our own voice speaks to us. It's easy to confuse our own desires with the voice of God. Third, the pressure we feel from others can be mistaken for the voice of God. When I was a professor, it was not uncommon for a senior student to drop out of seminary, and say, "I've never been happy here. I don't want to be a preacher. I finally realized that God hadn't called me here; it was the pressure I felt from my parents to be a pastor that brought me here." Fourth, the devil speaks to us. He tempts (1 Corinthians 7:5), lies (Acts 5:3), deceives (Revelation 20:8), teaches false doctrine in the church (1 Timothy 4:1), does counterfeit miracles (2 Thessalonians 2:9), and accuses us, especially when we pray (Revelation 12:10).

I hear the accusing voice of Satan all the time. Every time I stand onstage and pray for God to show me whom he will heal or to whom he wants to give a special message, I think, *I should have fasted for this meeting, or, I should have fasted more. I should have prayed more.* Or I might hear in my mind, *You just want God to heal people so they'll think you're awesome.* And there is some truth—actually a lot of truth—in all these accusations, so it doesn't do any good for me to argue for my goodness. Satan wants us to believe that God's goodness is contingent on our goodness so that we will feel it's useless to pray until we improve our performance. The apostle John saw that we overcome Satan's accusations by the power of the blood of the Lamb (Revelation 12:11), not by the power of our purity. In my spirit, I say back to the accuser, *I am a blood-bought son of the living God. Jesus will heal and deliver people today through the power of his blood, not through my goodness.* That usually silences the accusing voice and allows me to return to listening to the voice.

The most amazing thing I know is that God loves us and speaks to us. An eternal, omnipotent, omnipresent, omniscient Person—infinite in every way I can imagine and in ways I can't imagine—speaks to a small, arrogant, frequently ungrateful person like me. Why? There's only one possible answer to that question. He speaks to me because it gives him pleasure to talk with me.

God wrote his children a perfect book no one can master—not even a Saint Paul or a Saint Augustine. There was a time in my foolish youth when I believed that God's book was so great that God no longer needed to speak directly to us, for his book now did everything that God's voice used to do for us. Eventually, I came to see that I loved the Bible more than I loved God. I didn't love the Bible too much; I loved God too little. I saw that God would never let his book steal from him the pleasure it gave him to speak directly to the children he loves. God does not speak to us because he needs to; he speaks to us because he *wants* to.

When I had God locked into his book, I depended on my discipline to navigate through a stark world of black-and-white. When I let him out of his book, the pleasure of hearing his voice and feeling his love brought me into a world of vibrant color where all things were possible.

The theological landscape is different now than it was thirty-five years ago when I first began to hear the voice. Most Christians no longer need to be convinced that God speaks outside the pages of Scripture. The question I'm most often asked is, "How do I know if what I hear is *God's* voice?"

Four Tests for Recognizing the Voice

God's voice will never contradict Scripture, for Jesus said, "Scripture cannot be set aside" (John 10:35).[1] But from the beginning of the church, people have gone against apostolic

---

1. Jesus also said no one was to violate the "least" of the commandments (Matthew 5:19). Some may object that God commanded Abraham to sacrifice Isaac (Genesis 22). Although no specific command against child sacrifice had yet been given, the order to kill Isaac certainly went against the character of God revealed up to that point in Genesis. But the command was a test, and God himself prevented Abraham from fulfilling it. We would be hard-pressed to come up with an example of God commanding someone to violate the true meaning of biblical revelation.

authority based on their alleged encounters with angels, their visions, and their prophetic gifts (Colossians 2:16–19). Paul confronted this problem in the Corinthian church when he warned them, "If anyone thinks they are a prophet or otherwise gifted by the Spirit, let them acknowledge that what I am writing to you is the Lord's command. But if anyone ignores this, they will themselves be ignored" (1 Corinthians 14:37–38). Paul and the other biblical authors knew they were writing Scripture and that all believers had to submit their subjective experience to the authority of Scripture.

The tendency to exalt our experience over Scripture continues to this day. People predict dates for the second coming, despite Jesus' statement that no one knows the date of his return. People justify divorce by telling themselves that God would rather that they be happy with a different spouse than that they obey the commands to be faithful to their spouse (Matthew 5:31–32; 1 Peter 3:1–7). People tend to do what they think will make them happy or famous.

God's voice *will* violate our erroneous interpretations of Scripture. For a decade, I assured my seminary students and my church that the Bible taught that God had withdrawn the "miraculous" gifts of the Spirit. I deified the Bible by making it equal to God's voice, and I made myself a high priest of biblical deism. I taught my students that the essence of pastoral ministry was teaching the Scriptures, preferably book by book, not in topical sermon series. Instead of sending a lightning bolt my way for the damage I did to my students and church members, God smiled at his know-it-all boy and set a date for me to hear him speak his first words to me outside of the Bible—Saturday afternoon, April 5, 1986.[2]

The second test deals with the character of the voice, for voices express character. When the devil accuses us of sin, he condemns us. He tells us that God will never answer our prayers until we do better. He wants us to stop praying and work on doing better because he knows *better* will never come.

Over time, the fruit of that voice is despair. That evil voice can't be stopped or changed by changing our behavior. I have been walking and stumbling with Jesus for fifty-six years, and that evil voice has not stopped speaking to me. But that mean voice does not trouble me anymore. I have learned to ignore it, even when its accusations are true.

I ignore the voice of despair and listen to the voice that amazes. When Jesus spoke at the synagogue in Capernaum, people were amazed (Mark 1:22; Luke 4:32). When Jesus completed the Sermon the Mount, the people were amazed (Matthew 7:28–29). When he spoke at the synagogue in Nazareth, the people were amazed (Matthew 13:54; Mark 6:2). When the Sadducees tried to trap Jesus, the crowds were amazed at the words of Jesus (Matthew 22:33).

---

2. I tell this story in chapter 8, pages 141–42.

At the Feast of Tabernacles, Jesus drew all the people to himself, and even his worst enemies were amazed at his teaching (John 7:15). But that did not stop them from sending the temple guards to arrest Jesus (7:32). Yet the guards came back empty-handed and said, "No one ever spoke the way this man does" (7:46).

Every time Jesus speaks to me, I am amazed. Amazed because I don't deserve it, amazed by the wisdom, beauty, and compassion of the voice. Amazed at his love when he corrects me. His corrections give me hope and draw me closer to him. The voice of Jesus never causes me to despair or feel worthless.

The third test concerns the fruit of the voice. Jesus said, "A good tree cannot bear bad fruit, and a bad tree cannot bear good fruit" (Matthew 7:18). James drew out the implications of the Lord's words when he wrote, "The wisdom that comes from heaven is first of all pure; then peace-loving, considerate, submissive, full of mercy and good fruit, impartial and sincere" (James 3:17). This list could be viewed both as the qualities and the fruit of the voice. The voice that spoke to me on that stage was calm and peaceful, and it also produced peace in me.

Sometimes the character and the fruit of the voice that speaks to us are immediately known. The voice is authoritative and produces instant peace and longing for God. But sometimes the true character of the voice is revealed over time. I've known people who repeatedly listened to a voice that said God was punishing them. They get in a car wreck, and the voice says that God caused the wreck because the car they bought was too expensive or because they loved the car too much. The fruit of that voice is despair. God disciplines all his children, but he does so in love, producing hope by the power of the Holy Spirit.

The fourth test is that the voice is different from our voice. God says, "My thoughts are not your thoughts, neither are your ways my ways . . . As the heavens are higher than the earth, so are my ways higher than your ways and my thoughts than your thoughts" (Isaiah 55:8–9). Usually when God speaks to me, the voice seems to come out of nowhere and often introduces a subject I wasn't even thinking about and expresses a view different from mine. This is one of the ways I know I did not make up the voice.

When God said to me on April 5, 1986, "You are a deceiver and a manipulator, and you're just playing at church," I knew I never would have made that up. Why? Because it was the opposite of what I thought of myself. In print, those words look like an angry, harsh condemnation. But there was no anger in the voice when I heard God speak. It wasn't a condemnation. It felt like an invitation. It was as though God had said, "I've seen your ministry. If you want, I'm ready to show you *my* ministry." And with the voice came an implicit understanding. I "knew" I was standing at the crossroads of my life, and the way I responded to the voice would determine the course of the rest of my life. All I said was, "Yes, Lord." With that simple confession, I stepped onto the road to becoming a friend of God, though I didn't know it at the time.

I had been a deceptive shepherd convincing people that God no longer healed or spoke outside of the Scriptures, that our feelings are bad, that our reason alone can be trusted, that our theology was the best, and worst of all, that we were superior to other Christians. And it turned out that I was standing at a crossroads. A year after I said, "Yes, Lord," I was asked to leave my church—the church I led and had started with my best friends—and was fired from my seminary, my home for almost two decades. Some of my closest friends mourned this new direction, thinking I had plunged off a cliff into the syrupy seas of existentialism.

These four tests—scriptural agreement, godly character, good fruit, and exhibiting thoughts different from ours—can be helpful in the beginning, but they are not the definitive means of recognizing the voice of God. The more we ask God to speak to us, the more we will hear his voice. The more we hear his voice, the more we will recognize its character. The voices we know the best are the ones we listen to the most because they are the ones we love the most. The author of Hebrews explained it like this: "Solid food is for the mature, who by *constant use* have trained themselves to distinguish good from evil" (Hebrews 5:14, emphasis added).

When we are born again, we are given a capacity to

understand the voice of God, for Jesus said that his sheep hear his voice (John 10:1–18). This spiritual discernment allows us to hear God explain Scripture to us (Psalm 119:18) and to direct us in the details of our lives (Proverbs 3:6; Romans 8:14; see Psalm 139:24). Spiritual discernment is similar to our bodily strength in that the more we exercise it, the stronger it grows. This is what the author of Hebrews meant by "constant use."

You would think that if God spoke in an audible voice, everyone would recognize it. But that isn't true. A huge crowd had gathered around Jesus and heard him pray:

"Father, glorify your name!"

Then a voice came from heaven, "I have glorified it, and will glorify it again." The crowd that was there and heard it said it had thundered; others said an angel had spoken to him.

Jesus said, "This voice was for your benefit, not mine."

John 12:28–30

God spoke to Jesus in an audible voice, and some only heard thunder, even though God was speaking for the benefit of the crowd. This story shows that the key to recognizing the voice lies in the human heart, not in the form the voice uses.

For those who love God, an impression of the Spirit

can be as powerful as the audible voice of God. At Miletus, in Paul's farewell to the elders of the church at Ephesus, he said, "And now, *compelled* by the Spirit, I am going to Jerusalem, not knowing what will happen to me there. I only know that in every city the Holy Spirit warns me that prison and hardships are facing me" (Acts 20:22–23, emphasis added). The word translated "compelled" is the Greek verb *deo*, which normally means "to bind." Paul uses it in Romans 7:2 to say that "by law a married woman is *bound* to her husband" (emphasis added). For Paul, an impression of the Holy Spirit was as binding as the law. The ones who revere the voice like this are the ones who will hear it the best, even when the voice is leading them to lay their life down for Jesus.

Eventually, I would become a spiritual coach, teaching people of all ages how to hear the voice of God, how to discover their spiritual gift—especially how to heal and prophesy. One of the great blessings of my life today is to stand on a stage with my spiritual sons and daughters and watch them transform lives by the power of the Holy Spirit. But the blessing that transcends all blessings is hearing God say, "I love you." He says it in so many creative ways, in ways I never could have made up, in ways that make me feel like the most special person on earth. This is the greatest miracle I know. I am loved by an infinite Person who loves to tell me so.

Chapter 12

Getting Started

Sometimes God raises up sovereign vessels who seem to hear his voice effortlessly from the beginning of their ministries. Some biblical examples are Moses, Samuel, John the Baptist, and the apostle Paul. John Paul Jackson was one of the prophets I knew who heard God speak to him regularly from childhood. When he was five or six, he had a vision of one of his neighborhood friends killed in a car wreck. He ran to his mother and said, "Johnny is dead!"

"No, honey, he's not dead. He's playing right outside," she said. She pulled back the curtains, and there was Johnny playing next door. Two weeks later, Johnny was killed in a car wreck, exactly as John Paul had seen. He told me that when he was a young boy, he often knew what the adults around him were thinking. "That must have been a kick!" I said.

"No, it was awful. I couldn't understand why these people I loved didn't love one another. Though they would not say what they felt, they frequently had unkind thoughts about each other," he replied. John Paul was raised in a Christian home and in a denomination that had a theoretical belief in contemporary prophecy but no practical use of the gift. He didn't get the best use of his gift until he became part of a prophetic community.

Prophets like John Paul are rare. Most believers start out having never or only rarely heard the voice of God for themselves. Then something happens to them that makes them want to hear God speak personally to them. John Wimber called this event a "paradigm shift." I went through a radical paradigm shift that involved seven phases:

1. I studied Scripture to learn it is normal for God to speak to his followers, not an exception.
2. I studied Scripture to learn how God speaks.
3. I believed that God would speak to me.
4. I prayed for God to speak to me. In the New Testament, the believers asked God to grant them supernatural power to be his witnesses, and he answered their prayer (Acts 4:29–31). God is still answering these kinds of prayers when his children pray them diligently.
5. God sent me a coach to teach me how to hear God's voice.
6. I became part of a community that believes God speaks today and regularly practices hearing his voice and uses the gift of prophecy. I didn't hear the voice regularly until I became part of a community like this. Although there are exceptions, such as

John Wimber, most people I know who hear the voice of God learned to do so in group settings.

7. I took risks and embraced the fact that looking foolish in front of people is a non-skippable part of the learning process. The believers who go on to hear the voice well and have greater power in the kingdom suffer more than anyone else. This is the apostle Paul's regular testimony (1 Corinthians 4:9–13; 2 Corinthians 11:16–33; 12:7–10; 2 Timothy 3:12). Jesus taught his apostles that the price of apostolic power was incredible suffering (Luke 21:12–19).

I don't think there is one absolute way for everyone to learn how to hear the voice, but I have found that some version of the seven elements listed above is normal. The catalyst for my paradigm shift was a phone conversation with one of my heroes whom I had never met, the British professor of psychiatry and leading Christian author, Dr. John White. He was the first intelligent, highly educated, and biblically literate person I had ever met who believed God was still healing and speaking. That conversation provoked me to study the voice in the New Testament, and that study caused me to believe in the voice and to pray for God to speak to me.

I knew what it was like to have a spiritual coach. When I came to Dallas Seminary, three great scholars became my coaches in understanding Scripture. They taught me how to study the Scripture with precision. They were the greatest exegetes I had ever known. They gave me exegetical skills in Hebrew and Greek that I never would have developed on my own.

When I came to believe that God was still speaking and healing in his church, the Lord sent John Wimber to be my spiritual father and coach in the gifts of the Spirit. The summer before my seminary fired me (1987), Leesa and I went to a conference of more than three thousand people at John's church, The Vineyard Christian Fellowship of Anaheim. After a morning plenary session, the prayer team was praying for a hundred or more people at the front of the auditorium. Wimber stood on the stage and said, "There is a woman here who has cancer, and you have not come forward. Please come down to the front so we can pray for you." No response. He continued, "You flew in on Tuesday. You came here to be prayed for. Let us pray for you." No response. He said, "You're sitting in the back, and you're wearing a pink dress." A woman wearing a pink dress got up from the back row and walked up to the prayer team.

Afterward, I said to John, "That was amazing. That must have gone off like a foghorn in your mind."

"No, Jack. It was just the opposite. It was so faint I almost missed it. I was ready to walk off the stage, and I had the slightest impression that we were supposed to pray for a woman with cancer."

"What about the flying in on Tuesday?"

"When no woman came forward, I thought I should wait a moment longer. 'Tuesday' just floated through my mind. A lot of people come in a couple of days before the conference to enjoy Southern California. I thought that's what 'Tuesday' meant."

"Pink dress sitting in the back?"

"Well, when she didn't come forward, I saw pink floating over the back of the auditorium for a couple of seconds."

"John, you called out a woman in front of three thousand people because of those flimsy impressions?"

"Jack, I do it all the time. That's just the way God speaks to me when I'm praying for people. I've had better luck adjusting to his way of speaking than trying to get him to adjust to my way of hearing."[1]

I had read the biblical examples of God speaking to Isaiah or to Paul, but I had always assumed those communications came with the unmistakable clarity of an audible voice. I had learned how to discern the subtle nuances of certain biblical words in their original language, and I knew a great deal of skill was required to understand some of the biblical texts. But I never thought the voice of heaven would clothe itself in those gossamer impressions I had trained myself to ignore. I had never imagined it would take every bit as much skill to decipher the voice as it did to excavate a text like Hebrews 6:1–8. That is why God sent me a great coach.

---

1. I also tell this story in *Why I Am Still Surprised by the Power of the Spirit* (Grand Rapids: Zondervan, 2020), 36–37.

In those early conferences, every time I was around John Wimber, he taught me something new about hearing God's voice and about the healing ministry of the Holy Spirit. John told me that in his church, weekly home groups were the place where people learned how to hear God, discover their spiritual gifts, and become proficient at using their spiritual gifts. I asked John, "Do you think if I started a home group in my church that God would speak to us?" "Well, Jack, I don't know why he wouldn't," John replied.

With that encouragement, I started a home group in my cessationist church.[2] About twenty people came. The goal was to learn how to hear God's voice and learn how to pray for healing. We were all conservative evangelicals who had been cessationists until recently. At the beginning of the group, I taught for only twenty minutes on a practical aspect of hearing God's voice. I had so little voice that I plagiarized one of John's conference messages. The idea was to spend more time practicing hearing God's voice than talking about hearing his voice.

Then it was time to practice hearing his voice. I said to the group, "We're all beginners. The only way to learn to hear God's voice is by being willing to fail. The only good athlete you'll ever see is a bad one who didn't give

---

2. A "cessationist" believes that God has ceased giving the gifts of healings, miracles, and prophecy. Radical cessationists like I used to be believe that God no longer speaks except in Scripture. By asserting this, they think they are protecting the unique authority of Scripture when they are actually contradicting Scripture.

up." I wanted to create an environment where there was no shame in failure, where we could even laugh at our failures while we celebrated someone else's successes. I figured most of us would fail.

Then I prayed for God to speak to us about someone or some condition that he wanted to heal. We all bowed our heads and waited in silence for God to give us an impression or a picture of something he wanted to heal. Immediately, I had an impression that someone in the room had pain in their left elbow. After a few minutes, I asked, "Anybody feel like God may have spoken to them?" I decided for the time being that I wouldn't say anything about my elbow word.

A woman said, "I saw a picture of a right foot from the ankle down."

"Anybody have anything wrong with your right foot or ankle?" I asked.

A man had sprained his right ankle and said it wasn't healing properly. Somebody else gave a word, and it was wrong. I decided to wait a little longer on my elbow word. More people spoke up. Almost half the people who spoke up that night had seen an accurate picture or had a true impression. I held on to my elbow word. I told myself I was not being a hypocrite or trying to project the image of an awesome prophet who could not fail in front of people. I reasoned that if I, the leader, gave a wrong word, it would discourage everyone else. So out of my desire to protect God's people, I wasn't going to risk failing with my elbow word.

A couple of people we prayed for felt they were healed. Most weren't healed. But everyone loved the meeting. God had spoken and healed in our little group. He had done something we had never seen before. And that was the beginning of our journey into the gifts of the Spirit.

Later that night, Leesa and I sat in our den. I said, "Leesa, I had an impression that there was someone in the meeting with pain in their left elbow, but I was afraid to say it." She exploded in laughter. "I had the same word, but I was afraid to say it," she said.

Before I went to bed, I apologized to the Lord for my cowardice and hypocrisy. I was worried he might cast me on to the trash heap of hypocrisy and never speak to me again. "Lord, I promise if you'll speak to me again, I will never chicken out again." Then I asked, "Lord, would you show me who it was that had the pain in their left elbow?"

The next morning, my ten o'clock appointment walked through my church door, and I "knew" she was the "left elbow pain" woman. I asked her, "Glenda, did you have pain in your left elbow during the meeting last night?"

"Yes. It was killing me. Did you see me rubbing it?" she asked.

"Not exactly. Is it still hurting?"

"No. It was amazing. Nobody prayed for me, but when we started praying for others, my elbow pain left."

I pretty much kept my vow to God. I have looked foolish on stages all over the world. But I've become quite skilled at covering my failures with humor.

Soon, our Tuesday night home group became our favorite part of the week. The Holy Spirit was meeting with us. God surprised us every time we met. One night, someone had a word about God wanting to heal a fever blister. There was a visitor in the meeting that night. I saw him roll his eyes and suppress a sneer at the "fever blister revelation." But there was one person there who had a fever blister. I volunteered to pray for him. The living room was so crowded that we went into a bedroom to pray, just the two of us. He told me he had gotten the fever blister through a sexual sin. He was sure he had ruined his life. He hadn't confessed his sin to anyone. That night, he found forgiveness and hope through the Holy Spirit, and he returned to the Lord. I am continually amazed at the gentleness and kindness of the Lord.

After a few months, I knew who had gifts of healing, who had prophetic gifts, who had the gift of helps, and so on. And then there was an unsought, unexpected blessing. We had focused on enjoying the Lord and had become friends with one another. Without conscious effort, we had come to enjoy the "fellowship" of Acts 2:42. We had lunches and dinners with one another and shared our secrets.

I formed healing teams from our home group. Leesa and I took appointments to pray for people in my church office on Mondays, Wednesdays, and Fridays. We had healing teams for each of those days. We prayed for emotional pain as well as physical pain. Eventually we began to receive prophetic words for the people we prayed for. Sometimes the power of the Lord would fall on the person for whom we prayed and a demon would manifest. If we couldn't make the demon leave, I would stop the prayer session and call John Wimber. He always knew what to do.

I had all my Hebrew classes moved to Tuesdays and Thursdays at the seminary, which made for long days in Dallas, but it gave me five days to pursue the gifts of the Spirit in Fort Worth. Eventually, seminary students came to my office for prayer. Often, they confessed their secret sins. Word leaked out, and I had a constant stream of students in my office. Regardless of our theology, there is deep longing in the family of Jesus to experience his presence and power.

By the spring of 1987, I prayed for people seven days a week, but still not in Sunday church services. And that is how I learned to hear the voice of God: with a group of friends, embracing a trial-and-error method of learning, not afraid to fail in front of one another, and constantly practicing.

This is the usual way people learn how to hear the voice of God. First, they come to believe that Scripture teaches that God is still speaking to his children and that it is normal for them to hear his voice. Then God sends them someone who can both teach and demonstrate how to hear God. Then they become part of a group that meets weekly and is dedicated to hearing God's voice and helping one another find their spiritual gifts. Then they practice, practice, practice hearing God's voice.

Every Christian can hear God's voice for themselves, but prophets regularly hear the voice of God for other people. A year or so after I began to hear God's voice regularly, God sent John Paul Jackson into my life to become my friend and mentor. Over and over, I watched people weep as John Paul prophesied over them. In the beginning of our friendship, I besieged him with questions about prophetic ministry. He had the humility and humor to share his blunders as well as his successes.

Early in his ministry, at the end of a meeting, he saw a black cloud with a dollar sign ($) in it over the head of a man standing in the back of the meeting. John Paul was sure the vision was from the Lord. He thought the meaning was obvious: there was sin in the man's finances. So he called out the man and told him he needed to repent of financial sin. The man did not argue with him, but after the meeting, the man and his pastor came over to John Paul and to Mike Bickle, who was John Paul's pastor at that time. The man's pastor asserted that there was no way there was even a hint of financial sin in the man's life. The pastor had known this man for a long time and said he owned his own company, was generous with the poor, and was one of the biggest givers in the church, living far below his means. The pastor was so convincing that John Paul apologized to the man.

But John Paul was certain the vision was real and that he hadn't made it up.

Three weeks later, an employee was caught embezzling money in that man's company. The vision *was* from the Lord. There *was* sin in the man's finances, but it was an employee's sins, not the owner's sins. The interpretation was partially right, but the application was wrong: accusing the man of sin in front of everyone. This experience taught John Paul not to reveal sins publicly and not to assume an interpretation was correct, even when it seems obvious. We need help from God at every stage of interpretation—to know if the dream or vision is from the Lord, to know how to interpret it, and to know how to apply it.

Eventually, I'd go on to train young people in prophetic ministry. Twenty years later, some of those young people who are in their forties now are still doing conferences with me and bringing their young prophetic disciples with them. I can't imagine living or doing ministry without being able to hear the voice for myself and others.

Eventually, I would go on to train young people in prophetic ministry. Twenty years later, some of those young people who are now in their forties are still doing conferences with me and bringing their young prophetic disciples with them. I can't imagine living or doing ministry without being able to hear the voice for myself and others. Since the day God told me I was just playing at church, I have been pursuing his power.

Paul said, "The kingdom of God is not a matter of talk but of power" (1 Corinthians 4:20). The first-century church was a praying church, and as a result, they experienced the power of God. How much power should we expect? I don't know. But I do know that God has never given me all the power I've wanted and asked for.

This seems to be the pattern in the New Testament. For every person an angel breaks out of jail, it seems more are sawn in two. I see the wisdom of God in the bridling of our power, for there was only one Person who had the character to bear the power of the Spirit without limit (John 3:34), and yet even he had to embrace sacrifice. And out of that sacrifice, our Father brought the greatest power that this earth will ever know—the power to re-create the heart so that we love God with all our heart, soul, mind, and strength, and our neighbor as ourselves. This is the goal of power.

Chapter 13

Pursuing Prophetic
Ministry in the Church

The only person who never needed any help chose twelve helpers. Why? There is only one answer to that question. He chose them for the pleasure it gave him to love them and to teach them to love what he loved. The church that Jesus founded was based on friendship with him and producing disciples like him (Matthew 28:18–20). After Jesus ascended to his throne, he sent the Holy Spirit to empower his apostles and give them spiritual gifts to build churches that build disciples.

The church of Jesus is a body, not an organization. No one person has all the gifts. We all need each other for the body to function effectively. God never intended to divide the body into ministers and those who merely attend services. We are all spiritually gifted, so we all are ministers. All of us are supposed to bring a gift to give away when the body comes together (1 Corinthians 14:26). These spiritual gifts are part of a brilliant plan to unify us and equip all of us to be more effective in loving one another (1 Peter 4:7–11).

Prayer releases the power of the gifts and guides us in the wise use of the gifts (1 Peter 4:7). The church in

Acts was devoted to prayer (Acts 2:42). Luke never offers a sermon on prayer, but out of twenty-eight chapters, twenty-three tell stories about the power of prayer.

There are twenty-one spiritual gifts. Yet God singled out one of them for preeminence in the body of Christ—the gift of prophecy (1 Corinthians 14:1). Isaiah called prophets the "eyes" of Israel (Isaiah 29:10), and the New Testament prophets are the eyes of the body of Christ.

Prophets *see the future and help us prepare for it.* Agabus came to the church at Antioch and predicted "a severe famine would spread over the entire Roman world." The believers at Antioch took up an offering and sent it to the church in Judea to help them survive the famine (Acts 11:27–30). Prophets also *see the present priorities of God* for the body and for individuals. Paul and Barnabas were sent on their first missionary journey by prophets in the Antioch church (13:1–3). Prophets *provide supernatural guidance* for the whole body and for individuals. Paul's prophetic word saved the 276 people with him on the ship to Rome (27:21–26, 30–32). Prophets *see our weaknesses and strengths* and *supply supernatural encouragement and strengthening* for believers (15:32). Prophets *reveal the secrets of unbelievers* in a way that leads them to come to Christ (1 Corinthians 14:24–25). But prophets are not the leaders of the body. God has given elders the wisdom to lead the body (1 Timothy 5:17).

My first encounter with John Paul Jackson made it impossible for me to ever be happy in a ministry that was not infused with the power of prophecy. Since that day, I have trained young people to move in the gifts of the Spirit, especially the gift of prophecy. I have found that the younger they are, the easier it is for them to see visions and to prophesy. Young people will take risks that older people won't, and no one can grow in spiritual gifts unless they are willing to fail publicly. People in their early twenties have come with me to do conferences in other countries. I have put them beside me on a stage in front of thousands and watched them prophesy over people in the audience, who then broke down in tears. After the meeting, more than one hundred people stood in line for hours waiting for prophetic ministry. There is a hunger to hear God speak, and Christians all over the world are starved for the supernatural ministry of the Holy Spirit. They want to believe there is more to our faith than listening to lectures about our obligations.

How God Speaks to Prophets

God speaks to prophets in the same ways he speaks to all believers—theophanies, angels, the audible voice, the internal audible voice, impressions, sensations, dreams, and visions. Though it is more normal for prophets to have dreams and visions than the rest of the church. All believers can hear the voice of God for themselves. What sets prophets apart is not how they hear God, but the fact that they regularly hear the voice of God for other people.

When I taught Isaiah in Hebrew to seminary students, I assumed Isaiah always heard God speak with the clarity of an audible voice, but I taught that no writer of Scripture wrote God's word by taking down some sort of mechanical dictation. Rather than speaking in an audible voice, the Holy Spirit produced impressions in the minds of the scriptural authors, and they knew these impressions were from God, and they knew they were writing Scripture (1 Corinthians 14:37–38). God gave the writers freedom to express those impressions in their own vocabulary and style. That is why the writing prophets are so different from one another.

Teaching Prophetic Ministry in the Church

When I was a cessationist, I assumed that supernatural ministry in the New Testament was orderly. I did not understand the implications of the universality of spiritual gifts. God intended for every Christian to be a minister because the Holy Spirit had given a spiritual gift to every born-again person to serve the family of God (1 Corinthians12:11; 1 Peter 4:10). These gifts made the church a powerful family. It also made the church a messy family that required frequent correction. How could it not be messy? No one learns how to use their spiritual gift without making a mess. The New Testament Epistles were basically written to correct messes in the church.

I was given the gifts of evangelism and teaching when I was born again, even before I knew there were spiritual gifts. I drove unbelieving friends away from God by trying to bully them into the kingdom. The Holy Spirit raised up wise spiritual fathers and mothers to gently correct my mistakes and messes. A growing church will always be a messy church. But somewhere along the way, we let the bureaucrats clean up the mess and take over the church. We traded a powerful church for a predictable church. Eventually the house of prayer became a house of lecture. Even though it was reduced in power, it was still a great church. It saved me and my family, and it gave me a spiritual father to disciple me, to teach me how to love the things that Jesus loves.

Another false assumption I had about supernatural ministry was that it could not be taught. I assumed that prophets automatically heard God perfectly. "Prophets" meant to me the great writing prophets: Isaiah, Jeremiah, Ezekiel, and Daniel. I did not think about the group of anonymous prophets that Samuel commanded (1 Samuel 19:20). Since Samuel led the group, he must have taught or coached the group of prophets in receiving and delivering messages.

The fact that a ministry is supernatural does not mean it can't be taught. Jesus taught his disciples how to teach, heal, prophesy, and do miracles. All the gifts of the Spirit are supernatural. The power for their use comes from the Holy Spirit, not from human brilliance. This does not negate the fact that people need to be taught how to discover their gift and how to use it. The gift of teaching is supernatural. Teaching is not explaining the Scripture; it is revealing the excellencies of the Trinity and the kingdom of God by the power of the Holy Spirit so that the revelation changes lives.[1] All ministry is meant to lead human hearts to worship God, and that can only be accomplished through the power of the Holy Spirit.

When I'm pastoring a church, I typically devote one night a week to training in the spiritual gifts. I use Scripture to teach what prophecy is, and then I demonstrate the gift by prophesying over people in the meeting. Then I use exercises that allow the participants to practice prophesying over one another. After a while, I can hand off that meeting to young people who have gifts of teaching, prophecy, and healing.

I never use the Sunday morning service to allow beginners to practice their gifts. One of the quickest ways to teach church members to despise prophecy is to let beginning prophets—or, worse, those who don't even have a prophetic gift—hurl empty or hurtful words at the Sunday morning crowd. We would never come to the worship service and say, "Okay, who would like to give the sermon this

---

1. I wrote a whole chapter (23) on the gift of teaching in *Why I Am Still Surprised by the Power of the Spirit* (Grand Rapids: Zondervan, 2020), 204–20.

morning?" The Sunday morning service is a time for the mature expression of the gifts.

However, there is no one right way to use prophecy in the church. The Lord will guide the elders to discern the best way for that particular church, and that way can change over time. The key is to always listen to the Lord to guide us in how to use his gifts.

In the last church I pastored, we had an exceptionally gifted team of prophetic folks, mostly in their early twenties. Just before I preached the morning message, I brought up two or three of them to prophesy. They were so gifted that often people clapped and cheered, but we had a persistent problem with visitors who did not understand spiritual gifts. Sometimes they were so unnerved by being singled out in a crowd of people that they didn't know they couldn't even hear the content of what was being said over them. Because so many visitors had been attending, we stopped prophesying from the stage. Instead, we developed three-person teams that spent ten-minute sessions with three different people after the service. People signed up for prophetic ministry before the service. Each session was digitally recorded, and a copy was given to each participant, who then was free to contact the team with any questions they had about the sessions. Occasionally, we brought up someone who had been prophesied over to tell the whole church on Sunday what a blessing the ministry had been to them. It became our most popular ministry.

Most of the prophetic ministry in our church was done in our home groups. But the boldest and most gifted prophetic people constantly looked for ways to practice their gifts, just as the great evangelists are always looking to share the gospel with anyone they meet. Five of our prophets in their early twenties met for lunch frequently and had "contests" to see who could prophesy first over the server. This was far more than a game, for they led some of these servers to Christ and gave significant directions to others. At one lunch, Michael Rowntree said to the young woman waiting on them, "Sometimes the Lord speaks to me about people. I think he gave me a message for you. Would you mind if I shared it with you?"

"Please do," she said.

"I think the Lord is showing me that you and your mom are in a major conflict over the guy you're going out with right now."

"That is amazing. We are fighting. Do you know what I should do?" she asked.

Michael *did* know what she was supposed to do, but he didn't know how to tell her in a way that she could accept.

"Let me pray about that and see if the Lord will give me some advice for you," he said.

She went behind the curtain in front of the kitchen. When she came back to serve them, they could tell she had been crying.

After the meal, she asked Michael if the Lord had shown him anything more.

"I think so. If the young man is bringing you closer to Christ, then it's fine for you to stay with him. But if he's not, your mom is probably right."

This was a typical lunch with these young prophets. Three of the five went on to become pastors. They still travel with me across the country and internationally, doing conferences on friendship with Jesus and the gifts of the Spirit. They are in their late thirties now, equipping and training their own churches in the gifts of the Spirit.

A few years ago, I wrote *Even in Our Darkness*, my unsanitized story of becoming a friend of God. We preachers have a gift for standing onstage and sanitizing our stories, presenting a wonderful version of ourselves that only exists in our dreams. This makes our hearers think they are living unusually defective lives, and they go underground with their sin, and their sin flourishes in the darkness. I don't do that anymore. I share my struggles, and when I do, I see hope light up the eyes of my listeners. I have great editors at Zondervan. I wouldn't trade them for any other editorial group. They loved my story, but some Christian stores refused to carry my book when they learned it had profanity and other sins described in it. Our negotiations and discussions on what to include or cut were bogging down, and I was despairing of getting the book published. I felt like I was running out of time. Then on February 21, 2017, I received a text from Jeremy, one of the young pastors I had trained to prophesy, who was pastoring his own church by then. He asked some of the young people he was training to prophesy to pray and see if the Lord would show them anything about his friend. He did not tell them my name or profession or anything else about my circumstances. Here's what one of the young women sent him:

> I saw a guy signing books in a bookstore with a blue pen. The book cover has a sunset on it. I keep hearing this song I used to sing to my nephew when he was having a really difficult emotional day, and the words are, "Just one step and the next and then the next step and then the next. Flip your frown into a grin at day's end. We will win. We will win." I also keep hearing a tick of the clock. Your friend needs to know that time is on his side.

There was more to her word that was relevant for my situation, but it's not appropriate for me to share it. "Blue" for us has always meant revelation from heaven. The cover of the book had not yet been finalized, but it ended up being a west Texas sunset. I had been having an emotional day. But as soon as I read her word, the war in my soul ceased. All those voices presenting me with a cavalcade of bitter contingencies were vanquished by the one small, quiet voice that rules the world. Jesus said that in the world we will have trouble, but in him we will have peace (John 16:33). The word of a young woman I have never met took me out of the world and set me at rest in Jesus. I calmed down and waited. My editors were able to adjust the manuscript as I desired, and we were all happy.

It turns out that one of the unintended blessings of my training of prophets has been being on the receiving end of prophetic words that have enriched the lives of my family and me.

Prophetic Mistakes

People who are new to the gifts of the Spirit sometimes have difficulty in seeing how a contemporary prophet could make a mistake or get a revelation partially wrong, since the revelation comes from God.[2] It is true that all revelation from God is perfect, but this revelation must be interpreted and applied. I believe that Scripture is inerrant revelation from God, but my interpretation of Scripture is not inerrant, and even worse, sometimes my application of Scripture is hurtful. There is and will forever be only one perfect Teacher, Prophet, and Healer.

For the first part of my walk with God, I had no idea that Jesus wanted to be friends with me. I taught that God was no longer speaking or healing and that what was most important to God was improving the quality of our service

---

2. See appendix 3, a discussion of Deuteronomy 18:14–22, for an explanation of how a prophet can make a mistake.

so he could give us a better life. I taught these lies for years, but that didn't make me a false teacher. I still led people to the Lord during that time. False teachers teach lies to lead people away from God and induce them to follow Satan.

Today I can't imagine doing any version of life or ministry without hearing God's voice, without his specific guidance.

Before I lead a meeting, I ask God to guide me in teaching, healing, and prophesying. I don't hear an audible response, but I receive impressions about what we're supposed to do in the meeting before we ever get to the meeting. Sometimes God doesn't speak to me about the ministry time until I'm standing on a stage waiting for the Lord to speak before I pray for people.

My younger prophetic friends do the same thing. They frequently come to a meeting with no idea whom they are supposed to prophesy over. While I am teaching, they may stand in the back of the room praying and looking at the audience. When they find themselves drawn to an individual, they often receive impressions about that person. The impressions seem to come out of nowhere. Then they must interpret those impressions. Sometimes the impressions are clear, but sometimes they struggle to interpret the impressions. If they don't get an interpretation, they may tell the person the impression they received and ask if it means anything to them.

In October 2021, Michael Miller and I were leading a

conference on supernatural ministry in Statesville, North Carolina, hosted by Charles Burleson, pastor of Faith Church. During the ministry, we stood on the stage, and Michael said to a woman in the audience, "I see you sitting at a brown desk with a green lamp on it. You are poring over your Bible and taking notes. You want to make sure all that you believe and all that you teach agree with Scripture."

The woman, whose name was Sherry, said, "That is amazing. I haven't had that desk or lamp for years, but that was where I studied the Bible for years."

"The Lord is commending you for your hunger for him and your desire to believe only the truth in your pursuit of him." The fact that Michael saw a scene from years ago meant that Sherry had been faithfully pursuing the Lord for years, and the Lord wanted to commend her publicly in front of her friends.

Then Michael asked, "Do you have problems with your kidneys and skin?"

"No," she said.

I talked to Sherry after the ministry time. Her spirit was still dancing on the stars of God's affirmation. But some of the people who heard the prophetic word wondered how God could be its author when only 50 percent of it was correct. However, if we disagree with 50 percent of a teacher's explanation of a biblical text, it doesn't make us doubt the authenticity of the revelation of Scripture. We simply doubt the accuracy of part of the teacher's explanation of the

Scripture. We should listen to prophets with the same grace. It turns out that a woman named Jessica was sitting right behind Sherry, and she did have kidney and skin issues. Both impressions Michael had were true, but they applied to two different women. His mistake was to conflate them.[3]

Prophetic Healing and Evangelism

At the same conference in Statesville, after Michael prophesied over Sherry, he called out Mike, a man in his late thirties on the other side of the room. He said, "I see you leading young men. You also have knee pain due to the wear and tear of running. And I saw you kneeling down to fix a flat tire recently."

Mike seemed amazed. Michael asked him what the prophetic word might mean to him. Mike said he ran a business where he was overseeing several young men and mentoring

---

3. Later, Jessica was prayed for, but she was not healed. I talked to Pastor Charles a couple of weeks after the conference, and Jessica still hadn't been healed. This fact raises the question of how could God direct us to pray for someone's healing and then not heal them? Unless God tells me the reason, I don't know. Sometimes prayers aren't answered because of unbelief. Sometimes there's a timing issue involved that we don't see. So the Lord wants us to continue in prayer before he answers. God directs us to pray daily for his kingdom to come and for his will to be done, on earth as it is in heaven. His followers have been doing that for two thousand years, and he hasn't answered it yet. The truth is that we feel led to pray for things all the time without seeing our requests answered. But I see enough healing everywhere I go that I am still enthusiastic about praying for healing.

them. He did have severe knee and ankle problems from years of wear and tear due to running. The last detail was the most significant of them all. A while back, he had to learn how to change a tire on his own newly purchased SUV. It was frustrating because it was a far more technical process than for any tire he had changed before. Sometime after that, he hurried home from work to be with his family. He saw a car pulled over on the median, with its emergency blinkers on. He felt a strong inclination to pull over and help the man, but he ignored the inclination and kept driving. He drove past a couple of exits and then turned around and pulled up behind the stalled vehicle. The driver was in despair because he couldn't figure out how to change the flat tire. He had the same SUV as Mike, who knew exactly what to do.

God was using a prophetic word to publicly commend Mike for his kindness to a stranger, but that is not the best part of the word. Mike had only been invited to the conference that afternoon. His oldest daughter didn't want to come. She walked into the conference a minute before Michael began prophesying over her father. She was starting weekly visits to a specialist because her eating disorder was shutting her body down. Because of the accuracy of the word given to her father, she came to Pastor Charles and a couple others for prayer. Through the Holy Spirit, they were able to discover the main cause of her eating disorder and pray for her to be healed. She had a full meal when she got home. The specialist saw her a few days later and told her that her body was recovering and she didn't need to come weekly anymore, only every other week. She's well on the path to healing.

At church on Sunday morning, a young man in his early twenties came up to see Michael, along with the man's cousin and uncle. He introduced himself by saying that he had come to last night's meeting and was skeptical about healing, even though he had knee pain. His uncle and cousin had encouraged him to come for prayer that morning. Michael put his hand on the painful area next to the medial collateral ligament. He hadn't received an official diagnosis but was wearing a knee brace. When Michael prayed, the young man said he could feel something moving in his knee. He moved his knee back and forth and said, "I just don't understand what's happening."

Michael said, "It seems like God is healing your knee. It is a sign to let you know that he genuinely wants to know you and have a relationship with you."

The young man told Michael the story of his rebellion. Michael led him in a prayer, asking God to forgive him. Michael commanded evil to leave him. The man trembled and felt evil leaving him. Then he gave his heart to Jesus. He is in church now, learning how to walk with Jesus.

I love to do healing and prophetic ministry like this at conferences or in church services, but there are other ways to deliver prophetic messages. Prophets may speak to an individual privately or over the phone. They may send a written message to someone. Some prophetic people don't receive anything from the Holy Spirit until they touch a person. Some prophetic people are phenomenal at interpreting dreams. Some seem to specialize in encouraging people in their present circumstances, while others are better at revealing a person's future. Some specialize in evangelism. Some prophets, like Michael, are also healers and frequently give prophetic words about healing. Some prophets can do all these things.

I've already mentioned that home groups are great places to learn how to do prophetic ministry. But occasionally, without any warning, God simply turns on the tap, and revelation flows into a person who had no training in prophetic ministry and wasn't praying to be a prophet. This happened to one of my friends, Tim Johnson. I first met Tim when he was an All-Pro defensive tackle for the Washington Redskins back in the 1990s. I had gone to a prophetic and healing conference in Houston in the spring of 1993, and Tim was at that meeting. He thought his football career might be over because of a chronic neck and back injury that wouldn't heal. One of the prophets called out Tim from the stage. He told Tim he had a career-ending injury but that God was going to heal him. The prophet, who knew nothing about professional sports, told Tim he was planning to change teams, but not to do it because the Lord had planned something wonderful for him right where he was at the time. Tim was completely healed, stayed in Washington, and had his best year in his football career. The Quarterback Club of Washington named Tim the most valuable Redskins player of the 1993 season.

Tim pastors a church now in Orlando. He gets up every day before sunrise to spend the first hours of the day in prayer. Since Tim became a Christian, he has been able to hear the voice of God giving him specific directions for his ministry, but he didn't hear prophetic words for other people, even though he loved the prophetic ministry.

Recently, without any advanced notice, God has begun to surprise Tim with amazing prophetic words for people, especially for people he has never met. The messages are long and detailed and seem to flow out of nowhere. Tim writes down the impressions until they cease coming.

On his morning prayer walk at 7:32 a.m. on September 14, 2021, Tim received a prophecy for Eugene Lockhart, a retired NFL player. Tim knew the player's name but nothing about his circumstances, and he had never met Eugene.

I was a die-hard Dallas Cowboys fan from the 1960s on and had watched Lockhart play linebacker for the Cowboys. He was the first rookie in Cowboys history to start at middle linebacker. In 1989, he set a club record and led the NFL in tackles (222). His ability to take pain and deliver pain earned him the nickname "Mean Gene, the hitting machine."

In the 1980s, before my fall from seminary grace, I was

friends with John Weber, who was the chaplain for the Cowboys. John was also a Dallas seminary graduate. At one of our lunches, he told me that he thought 80 percent of the NFL players crash and burn after they leave the NFL. They have no life coaches to help them adjust to life out of the limelight and the wealth of the NFL. Eugene was one who crashed. He was sentenced to four and a half years in prison for his role with eight others in a $20 million mortgage fraud scheme in Dallas. He was released in May 2015 after serving three years.

Here is the word Tim received for Eugene:

> Eugene is spiraling mentally, and he is spiraling emotionally. He does not know what to do. He does not know where to turn. Tell him to turn to me, and I will deliver him. I will set him free.
>
> If Eugene will trust the work my Son did on the cross for his deliverance, he will no longer hold on to unforgiveness, no longer hold on to his sin, no longer hold on to his past, no longer hold on to the shame, no longer hold on to the guilt, no longer hold on to the fear, no longer hold on to the voices telling him to kill himself and telling him he is worthless, no longer hold on to the anger, no longer hold on to the poverty in his soul, no longer hold on to the self-destruction of his life and of his family's life that has ruled his life for many years. I have called him to live in my Son, to love him,

to trust him, to live for him, to enjoy him, to never walk away from him.

I will anoint Eugene with the gift of evangelism to preach my word to those who live in darkness, to those who live in the prison of false freedom bound by Satan and bound by the demonic strongholds of the enemy that I will set him free from. I will break every chain in his life. I will let my Spirit come on him to break chains in the lives of those I send him to and in the lives of those I send to him.

He must know this is his last chance to give me his *whole heart*. The enemy has desired to destroy him completely. I have had mercy on Eugene all of his life. I have been patient to let Eugene come to my Son, to trust him for the forgiveness of his sin and to trust him for a new life, for resurrection life to flow in him and through him. If Eugene rejects my Son, the enemy will rightfully have his way to completely destroy him, to mock my purpose for him, to drag him into the lake of fire in eternity.

I have loved Eugene with an everlasting love. I will never give up on him. I sent my Son to rescue him, to show him who I am. I am his heavenly Father who provides, who protects, who guides, who covers his children. I will not force Eugene to trust my Son to save him. I will not stop the enemy's plan if he says no to me. Eugene, are you ready to say yes to me?

Abba

Tim prayed for Eugene for five weeks, asking God to open a door for the delivery of this word. At 7:00 p.m. on October 20, 2021, Tim called Eugene, introduced himself, and asked if he could read a message to him that he believed was from God. Eugene said yes.

Eugene was overwhelmed with God's love for him and wept for joy. He told Tim that every word of the message was true, that he had been running from God since he was twelve, and that he had been crying the whole day, so hard at one point that he had to pull off the freeway. That night, Eugene stopped running from God and gave his heart to Jesus. Tim prayed for Eugene, and Eugene could feel the power of God come on him.

Tim never saw himself as a prophet. He honored prophets but never pursued a prophetic ministry. His main love was pastoring God's children and introducing people to Jesus. Yet he receives these kinds of prophecies regularly. And every time he does, he is amazed by the grace of God. Maybe that's one reason why God can entrust Tim with such supernatural ministry.

Thirty-five years ago, when I was stumbling out of the prison of cessationism, I crashed into 1 Corinthians 14:1 (NIV 1984): "Follow the way of love and eagerly desire spiritual gifts, especially the gift of prophecy"—a trifold command in a single short sentence. In theory, I agreed with the first imperative, but I couldn't see what in the world spiritual gifts had to do with love, and the third imperative knocked me on my rump. I couldn't think of a better way to compromise the authority of the Bible and let chaos loose in the conservative church than to tell believers to start hurling prophetic words at one another. And sure enough, I've seen prophecy abused by well-meaning and not so well-meaning believers. But I've also seen preachers use sermons to lambaste their detractors. I've seen every good thing abused by believers. And I've done my share of abuse.

The way to stop abuse is to "follow the way of love." The spiritual gifts are the tools of love that the Holy Spirit uses to build up the body of Jesus. Discovering our spiritual gifts and using them under the direction of the Holy Spirit make us better lovers of God's people. Prophecy is God sharing his secrets with his friends and with those he wants to become his friends so that they supernaturally feel his great love for them. That's why God has told us to pursue prophecy above all the other gifts.

Chapter 14

The Purpose of
God's Gifts

The apostle Paul began his description of the greatest force in the world with a curious warning:

> If I speak in the tongues of men or of angels, but do not have love, I am only a resounding gong or a clanging cymbal. If I have the gift of prophecy and can fathom all mysteries and all knowledge, and if I have a faith that can move mountains, but do not have love, I am nothing. If I give all I possess to the poor and give over my body to hardship that I may boast, but do not have love, I gain nothing.
>
> *1 Corinthians 13:1–3*

When Paul wrote this warning, he had been walking with the Lord and the Lord's people for more than twenty years. Over and over again, he had seen the tendency of God's people to exalt the gifts of God over God himself. This is not a criticism of God's gifts. It is a testimony to the power and beauty of his gifts and a revelation of the weakness and impurity of God's people.

For the first seventeen years of my life, I believed in the existence of God but knew nothing about him or his gifts. I trusted Jesus to forgive me and give me a new life when I heard my first verse of Scripture—John 10:28—on December 18, 1965. That week, I began to devour Scripture.

Ten years later, I became a professor of Old Testament exegesis and Semitic languages. Somewhere in that journey, knowing the Bible became more important to me than loving the God of the Bible. The Bible replaced the voice of God in my life. I even taught my students that God no longer speaks to us outside the Bible.

Twenty years after I became a Christian, I repented of my bibliolatry. I no longer found my validation in my knowledge of Scripture, but rather in being a champion for the miraculous. Eventually, prophecy became the gift that most validated me. It happened when I met prophets who could tell me the secrets of my heart.

There was one prophet who would be used for both good and ill in my life. His name was Paul Cain, and I first met him in September 1987. I was thirty-nine years old, and he was fifty-eight, but he could have passed for seventy. He was frail, had heart problems, and was generally unimpressive. He did not show much knowledge of Scripture or theology. He had been involved in the Pentecostal healing revival of the 1940s and had some great stories to tell. When I met him, I thought he was at the end of his race. I couldn't imagine him moving in power like John Wimber and thought his main value was as a historical repository of a decade of miracles back in the healing revival.

Then we had our first meeting where we ministered together. After I spoke and gave a teaching, Paul got up and called out people, telling them their diseases and the secrets of their hearts and pronouncing some of the people to be healed. It was amazing. I introduced Paul to my new friends in Fort Worth who had international ministries and had recently been introduced to the gifts of the Spirit. At one meeting, Paul called out a woman and named five diseases that were afflicting her. It was all true. Then he pronounced her healed. I interviewed her soon after the meeting. She was completely healed.

None of us had ever seen a prophet or healer like Paul. But all of this power came in the frailest of packages. He was frequently sick and sometimes addled both on and off the stage. He had a full-time assistant who prepared all his meals and gave him his medicines and did a thousand other things for him.

Paul asked me to introduce him to John Wimber. I told John about him and tried to schedule a meeting, but it wasn't working out. Then in the summer of 1988, we moved to Anaheim with our three children to be on John's staff. In September of that year, I asked Paul when he was coming to Anaheim to meet John. He said, "I don't know yet. But the Lord shows that there will be an earthquake in Southern California on the day I arrive."

"An earthquake! The big one?" I asked.

"No. It won't be the big one. But on the day I leave Southern California, there will be a big one somewhere on the earth. The Lord hasn't shown me where," he said.

I told John about Paul's earthquake prophecy. He smiled, sort of a "been there, done that, heard all this before" smile.

Paul got on a flight to come to Anaheim on December 3, 1988. At 3:38 a.m. on December 3, 1988, my English Pointer, Skipper, hurled himself against the glass patio doors trying to get into the house, and then a 5.0 earthquake, centered under Pasadena, rumbled down the coast to Orange County and shook our house. That morning, John and I rode together to pick up Paul, and I reminded John of the earthquake prophecy that Paul had shared with me. "What kind of guy is this?" John said. "An earthquake is his calling card!"

Paul's visit to the Vineyard was so supernatural that he quickly came into John's inner circle and was invited to minister at all the major conferences. Paul returned to Dallas four days later, on December 7, and the big earthquake that he prophesied came to pass. On that day, two earthquakes struck Armenia just minutes apart. The first was a 6.9, and the second was a 5.8. Together, they killed at least sixty thousand people and destroyed almost half a million buildings. I had never heard of God authenticating a prophet like this. I thought to myself, *He must be special, the godliest prophet on earth.* And it made sense to me.

It would be just like God to put great power in the frailest of packages. Paul and I became close friends and did ministry together for sixteen years.

One of the warnings I had given people when I first came to believe in contemporary miracles was that the power of a person's spiritual gift was not an indication of their spirituality. And then I ignored that warning for myself. I had such confidence in my discernment and in my knowledge of Scripture and theology that I did not think I could be deceived.

From the beginning of our relationship, Paul told me that one day we would stand in stadiums filled with people and see resurrections. The emphasis was always on *we*. I believed him because I saw him do greater miracles and give more detailed prophetic messages to people than anyone in my experience.

Paul confessed to long-term sexual immorality and alcoholism in 2004. I do not believe Paul's sin invalidates the prophetic and healing blessings he brought to many people. After 2004, he never returned to prominence in ministry. He died at the age of eighty-nine on February 12, 2019.

I am telling you about my relationship with Paul, not to indict him, but to indict myself. Prior to 2004, I saw him regularly do things I would not permit my staff to do. When I confronted him, he always had an excuse. I let it slide because I believed Paul was going to take us into a special realm of power.

My fundamental error was not to heed the apostle Paul's warning in 1 Corinthians 13:1–3. I had thought primarily of Scripture, spiritual gifts, and self-sacrifice as a validation of ministry. They are not. They are gifts of God meant to express and produce love for God and for his people. Knowing this is a key to discerning spiritual prophets.

Spiritual Prophets, Carnal Prophets, and False Prophets

Spiritual prophets use their prophetic gift to lead believers to love God and to lead unbelievers to faith in the Lord.[1] There are carnal prophets, true believers with a true gift of prophecy, who use their gift to exalt themselves and who cause division in the body of Christ.[2] And there are false

---

1. Some cessationists argue that since all contemporary prophets admit to making mistakes—if the prophets are sane—there can't be any true contemporary prophets. They use Deuteronomy 18:14–22 to prove that true prophets can't make a mistake. But this is a baseless interpretation, one that no Hebrew scholar would ever support. See appendix 3 for an explanation of Deuteronomy 18:14–22 that is based on exegesis, not on theological convictions that have no exegetical support.

2. Paul was the spiritual father of the Corinthian church. When he wrote his first letter to them, he summed up their spiritual state by saying, "Brothers and sisters, I could not address you as people who live by the Spirit but as people who are still worldly—mere infants in Christ" (1 Corinthians 3:1). The Greek word translated "worldly" is *sarkinos*, which means "fleshly," that is, "weak, sinful, and transitory (Walter Bauer, *A Greek-English Lexicon of the*

prophets. There are two kinds of false prophets: unbelievers who use the devil's power and unbelievers who have learned how to traffic in the Lord's power.

By the end of the first century, John wrote that "many false prophets have gone out into the world" (1 John 4:1). Jesus had warned the apostles that false prophets, false teachers, and false christs would deceive many people, especially in the last days, by performing great signs and miracles (Matthew 24:11, 24). Satan supplies the power for them to do all kinds of counterfeit miracles, signs, and wonders (2 Thessalonians 2:9). False prophets and false teachers deny that Jesus is the Christ (2 Peter 2:1). The defining purpose of their mission is to lead people away from Jesus Christ by leading people to themselves.

At the end of the Sermon on the Mount, Jesus described

New Testament and Other Early Christian Literature, ed. Frederick W. Danker, 3rd ed. [Chicago: University of Chicago Press, 2000], 914). The KJV translated *sarkinos* as "carnal," the English word in 1611 for "fleshly." And "carnal" is still at home in the theological world of English speakers. All newborn Christians are carnal, just as all newborn babies are selfish. Given the right nourishment and good spiritual environment, baby Christians grow into spiritual Christians who produce the fruit of the Spirit (Galatians 5:22–23). The Corinthians should have become spiritual Christians by the time Paul wrote them, but they were characterized by jealousy, quarreling, and sexual immorality. The author of Hebrews had the same complaint about those who received his letter (Hebrews 5:11–14). Being born again does not guarantee spiritual growth. Our spiritual gifts don't guarantee our spiritual growth. It is possible to have a genuine spiritual gift of prophecy and remain a carnal prophet for one's entire life. Spiritual gifts are given, not earned. It is possible to have an impressive spiritual gift and remain a carnal believer all one's life. Samson had great power, but he never developed the character to use that power with wisdom.

the second class of false prophets—those who have learned how to utilize or traffic in the power of the Lord but who do not know him.

> "Not everyone who says to me, 'Lord, Lord,' will enter the kingdom of heaven, but only the one who does the will of my Father who is in heaven. Many will say to me on that day, 'Lord, Lord, did we not prophesy in your name and in your name drive out demons and perform many miracles?' Then I will tell them plainly, 'I never knew you. Away from me, you evildoers!'"
>
> *Matthew 7:21–23*

These prophets are not using Satan's power for their miracles. Satan will never supply power to drive out demons (Matthew 12:25–26). Although these prophets do not trust in Jesus, they have learned how to use his power to do miracles and to prophesy. They are like the evangelists who lead people to the Lord without ever having for themselves a saving relationship with the Lord.

Jesus said there are miracle workers who are so skilled masquerading as believers that many of them won't be revealed as unbelievers until the end of the age. Although their miracles will be a blessing to individuals on whom the miracles are performed, the Lord calls them "evildoers" because the overall effect of their ministries will be to draw people away from the Lord and to usurp the Lord's place in the lives of their followers. When the Lord says, "I never knew you," he means he does not recognize them as belonging to his family, as having a spiritual relationship with him.[3]

The fact that there will always be false prophets among us is not a reason to resist all prophetic ministry. There will always be false teachers among us, but no one uses that fact as an excuse to resist all teachers. There will always be carnal prophets and carnal teachers, people with true spiritual gifts who use their gifts to exalt themselves and draw people to themselves. Power is not the test for true ministry; love is. True ministry draws people to Jesus and produces love for Jesus and for the people of Jesus.

---

3. This is one of the meanings of the Greek word *ginosko* ("to know"); see Bauer, *Greek–English Lexicon*, 201:7.

Chapter 15

Guidelines to Avoid
Prophetic Traps

P aul Cain is a vivid example of a fact we must acknowledge. People can be very gifted, perhaps even gifted
to ministry in the Lord's power, and yet they are still sinful
men and women. Their gifting does not *excuse* their sin, and
it should not lead us to elevate them to a place where they
are unaccountable for their sin.

Like any of us, prophets are subject to sinful temptations. There are several traps that are common to those in
prophetic ministry, temptations they are especially prone to
fall into due to the nature of this ministry. They can fall prey
to bouts of jealousy and anger, the desire to please people
and to be applauded and lauded by crowds. Prophets who
minister with humility will seek out accountability and be
aware of their own shortcomings and seek to avoid some of
the most common mistakes and traps of prophetic ministry.

Prophesying Out of Jealousy and Anger

Prophets should never trust a "revelation" received about
someone with whom they are angry or jealous. Saul knew

what it was like to feel the Holy Spirit come on him in prophetic power (1 Samuel 10:10). He also knew what it was like for the Spirit of God to empower him for heroic action (11:6–11). Later in his life, Saul's jealousy of David drove him to rage (18:6–9). This is what happened to him during one of those periods of jealousy and anger:

> The next day an evil spirit from God came forcefully on Saul. He was prophesying in his house, while David was playing the lyre, as he usually did. Saul had a spear in his hand and he hurled it, saying to himself, "I'll pin David to the wall." But David eluded him twice.
>
> *1 Samuel 18:10–11*[1]

One of the most instructive things about this passage is the phrase used to describe the evil spirit: it "came forcefully." This is the same phrase in Hebrew that is used of the Holy Spirit coming on Saul in 1 Samuel 10:10 and 11:6. Another remarkable thing about this story is that when the evil spirit came on him, Saul began to "prophesy." This is the same word for prophesying used in 1 Samuel 10:10. I think the biblical author is telling us that when the

---

1. It may sound strange to some that God would use an evil spirit to accomplish his purposes. However, all power belongs to God whether human, political, or spiritual. He used evil nations like Assyria and Babylon to discipline his people. Why wouldn't he use evil spirits for the same purposes? This happened to Saul several times (1 Samuel 16:14, 15, 23; 18:10; 19:9). It happened to David (2 Samuel 24:1 and 1 Chronicles 21:1) and to others (Judges 9:23; 1 Kings 22:19–23).

evil spirit came on Saul and gave him demonic prophecy, Saul mistook it for the power and inspiration of God. His jealousy and anger caused him to mistake the power of an evil spirit for the power of the Holy Spirit.

The Desire to Please People

The apostle Paul wrote, "If I were still trying to please people, I would not be a servant of Christ" (Galatians 1:10). People-pleasing is a killer for all ministry, not just for prophetic ministry.

In the Old Testament, false visions and flattery go hand in hand (Ezekiel 12:24). When prophetic people give in to the pressure of telling people what they want to hear, they end up prophesying out of their own imaginations (13:2). The desire to please people leads a prophet, or any other leader, to ignore sin and give vain comfort (Lamentations 2:14; Ezekiel 13:15–16; Zechariah 10:2). In the worst case, this desire to please can open the door for a demonic spirit to speak through a prophet (1 Kings 22:6–28).

The Desire to Be Awesome

The desire to be awesome in ministry, to be "a prophet to the nations," is exactly opposite of the true spirit of prophecy. An angel told John, "The testimony of Jesus is the spirit of prophecy" (Revelation 19:10 ESV). Prophecy is meant to testify to the awesomeness of Jesus, not to the awesomeness of the prophet's ministry. The greatest prophets want people to behold the glory of Jesus. They care little about how they are viewed. John the Baptist was one of the greatest of all prophets because he said *and meant*, "He must become greater; I must become less" (John 3:30). People who feel like John the Baptist can be entrusted with great revelations.

Rationalizing Mistakes

Sometimes prophetic people rationalize their mistakes or simply refuse to admit they made a mistake. I don't know any prophetic people today who are 100 percent accurate. All prophetic people I know make mistakes, just as evangelists, teachers, pastors, or other Christian leaders do as well. Sometimes prophets mistake their own impressions for one of the Lord's impressions. Sometimes they make mistakes in interpreting and applying impressions the Lord gives them. Rationalizing or failing to admit mistakes is what usually ruins credibility. People trust people who say they were wrong. They can't trust those who won't admit they were wrong.

Making Economic Predictions

I think it's a good idea for prophetic people to avoid all financial predictions and leave the stock market, bond market, and real estate market to the experts in those areas. There are at least two reasons for avoiding these kinds of predictions. First, it cheapens prophetic ministry. God is raising up prophetic ministry to exalt Christ, not to enrich church members. Second, too often these predictions will be wrong, since the Holy Spirit is against using spiritual gifts for personal financial gain.

Ask God how to invest and spend your own money, but don't prophesy to others what they should do with theirs. You will probably be wrong.

Prophetic Gossip and Slander

If prophets tell a negative vision or impression to someone other than the person who was the subject of their revelation, they are most likely committing a sin. If the vision is true, the sin is gossip. If the vision is false, the sin is slander.

I have seen significant trouble caused by prophetic people who have revealed the sins of others and prophesied judgments on people without ever taking it up with the original people.

Calling Out Sins Publicly

Sometimes it is appropriate for a leader to deal with a person's sin publicly. Peter called out Ananias's and Sapphira's sin, and Paul called out Elymas's sin, and sometimes he named people's sins in his epistles. Paul even rebuked the apostle Peter publicly when Peter's hypocrisy compromised the gospel (Galatians 2:11–21). Likewise, elders who are sinning are to be publicly rebuked (1 Timothy 5:20). And when someone is disciplined by the church, it must be done in public (1 Corinthians 5:1–5). However, in the New Testament, public exposure of a believer's sins is reserved for extreme cases. The normal procedure is to go to a brother or sister privately and attempt to win them before there is ever a public exposure (Matthew 18:15–17; Galatians 6:1–2). Normally, you may never accuse someone of sin based on a private revelation. In the case of an elder, the church is not even allowed to entertain an accusation against the elder unless it is brought by two or three witnesses who have firm evidence (1 Timothy 5:19).

Once I was speaking to an audience of committed Christians, many of whom were leaders and pastors. At the conclusion of the meeting, I had an impression that a number of people in the audience were addicted to both prescription drugs and alcohol. My attention was drawn to a small section in the back of the room. I said, "I think the Lord will help some people today who are struggling with an addiction to prescription drugs and alcohol. If you'll stand up where you are, we'll pray for you now." Then I pointed to the section in the back and said, "There is someone in this section who needs help." Immediately a man stood up, and then people in every section began to stand.

I think this is an appropriate way of publicly naming sins. It gives a person the opportunity to choose to make a public confession. It also does this in a way that says to them, "We want to help you, not embarrass you." People frequently write me to say they repented and were delivered of sins in meetings like this.

A word of caution, however. I don't do this often. The church is filled with sins. Anyone can stand up before a Christian audience and say, "The Lord shows me that some of you are committing the sin of . . . ," and accurately name sins present in the audience. But if the Lord is not leading someone to name those sins, not much good will come of that "ministry" and, in fact, significant harm may follow. Naming sins takes no gift at all. The key is knowing what particular sin the Lord wants named—if he wants it named at all—and when, where, and how he wants to deal with the sin. He gives grace to deal with these things when he is leading. We usually get frustrated and cause frustration when we are leading.

Every time I stand before an audience, I have to fight the desire to be seen as awesome. I have to remind myself the audience that counts is above me, not in front of me.

I have to pray every day that God will grant me grace to stand on a stage, driven by grace to honor Jesus and help his people.

The "God Told Me" Trap

All of us who believe that God is still speaking will "hear" him tell us to do something that is embarrassing. One of my friends who has a significant healing gift heard God tell him to pray for a man in a wheelchair in the supermarket. This event happened at the beginning of his healing ministry. The wheelchair man said, "No." My friend chased him down the supermarket aisles, trying to get him to change his mind. The first time anyone prays for a person who is deaf, mute, or blind, they usually struggle with whether or not they should put their spit on the person because that's the way Jesus prayed (Mark 7:33; 8:23). My general rule is that if it seems God is telling a beginner in healing and hearing God to do something that would embarrass the person they're praying for, don't do it. God will understand. There is a huge difference between doing something that will only embarrass us and doing something that will embarrass the person for whom we are praying. God did command his prophets to do some weird things, but those prophets weren't beginners in hearing the voice of God.

Give a Word and Then Pray

Once we deliver a prophetic message, our job is over—except to pray. If our advice is not taken, we shouldn't feel rejected. Nor should we feel that those who refuse our advice are in the grip of evil or are hard-hearted. In time, everything may work out just fine. Or it may be that we will see it wasn't the Lord speaking to us at all or that we had significantly misunderstood what he was saying. Perhaps we were just one in a series of confirmations to help a friend or a leader change courses. The prophet's job is to deliver the word, not to try to make it happen.

Ask for a Specific Word
Rather Than Generalities

If I'm standing on a stage in front of a crowd and praying for healing, I know that many people in the room have back pain. That is not a revelation from God. So I don't start with general words for mass healing. I ask God to give me names of people and their specific conditions that he will heal. Or I'll look across the crowd, asking him to show me the pain of specific individuals. I will find myself looking at a woman, at the left side of her face, and the word *tinnitus* will pop into my mind out of nowhere. Then I ask her if she has tinnitus in her left ear. Usually she does, and usually she will be healed when we pray for her. Using specific revelation like this to pray for individuals raises the level of faith for healing in the crowd. I saw my spiritual father John Wimber pray for people like this, and I said, "Lord, please give me specific healing words for specific people." And he did. All I had to do was stand onstage and be willing to fail in front of people—fail a lot in front of people. When I first tried to use revelatory words to guide me in praying for the sick, I was wrong 99 percent of the time. I learned to make jokes about my failures. And my failures gave people in the audience courage to fail. And after a few years, I began to consistently receive specific words for healing. Nobody gets good at anything until they have failed a lot trying to do that thing.[2]

I was at the large church of a friend, and another pastor brought a prophetic team of young people from his church to prophesy over people in my friend's church. I sat in on one session. The young "prophets" said things like, "You're frustrated at work, but the Lord is going to heal that frustration. You are lonely now, but it is only for a season." They spoke for about fifteen minutes at this sustained level of generality without giving one specific revelatory word. None of them were willing to take the risk of giving a specific word that

---

2. I used to tell people that they if they wanted to move with consistent power in healing and prophetic gifts that they had to *be willing* to fail in front of people. But that was sugarcoating it. Those who want to move with spiritual power have to be more than *willing*; they have to fail in front of others over and over. There may be exceptions to this rule. If that encourages you, you probably won't be an exception.

could be immediately proved wrong. So there was no risk of anyone they prophesied over falling on their face and exclaiming, "God is really among you!" (1 Corinthians 14:25).

Sometimes at a conference, a speaker will bring up a prophetic team that will call out specific words, but they don't ask anyone to respond in a way that shows the prophet was right or wrong. I saw one "prophet" call out ten different conditions in rapid succession and say, "You who have those conditions come up afterward so we can pray for you." I suspect that person had a greater desire to be *perceived* as a prophet than to actually *be* a prophet. Always give public prophetic words in a way that allows them to be tested publicly—if you want to grow in your prophetic gifting.

Stay Off the Prophetic Bandwagon

In 1999, many prophets were prophesying the Y2K cataclysm. Computers all over the world were going to cease to function because their outdated software would not be able to recognize the year 2000. Prophets claimed the total collapse of society was imminent. I only knew two or three prophetic people who believed nothing would happen. But many "prophets" fueled the mass hysteria. Based on their predictions of doom and mayhem, people borrowed money to buy generators and guns. Someone asked me if I was going to buy a generator since I lived on a mountain in

Montana. I said, "Sure. I'm buying mine on January 2, 2000. They will be dirt cheap then."

I never heard a single prophet of Y2K doom admit they made a mistake. One prominent "prophet" attempted to cover up the blunder by saying that the church prayed and that's why the world did not end. That was so dishonest. I never once heard these prophetic doomsayers predict that the disaster could be averted through prayer. They all spoke of it as a decreed event. One thing this fiasco demonstrated was that a person can have a large prophetic ministry that siphons off a lot of money from the naive without being a prophet at all.

Another bandwagon picked up some steam in 2019. Many "prophets" prophesied that 2020 would be a great year of blessing and outpouring of the Holy Spirit. Instead, churches had to stop meeting in public, hundreds of thousands were killed by the pandemic, and the country reeled from political upheaval—and no prophets admitted they got it wrong. This lack of accountability is a serious setback for those of us who believe in the contemporary supernatural ministry of the Spirit.

The Contingent Nature of Prophecy

Often prophetic words are contingent on the actions of those who receive them. A key passage describing the contingent nature of prophetic words is Jeremiah 18:7–10:

If at any time I announce that a nation or kingdom is to be uprooted, torn down and destroyed, and if that nation I warned repents of its evil, then I will relent and not inflict on it the disaster I had planned. And if at another time I announce that a nation or kingdom is to be built up and planted, and if it does evil in my sight and does not obey me, then I will reconsider the good I had intended to do for it.

Jonah prophesied that Nineveh would be overthrown in forty days. But the entire city called on God, fasted, and repented. God had compassion on them and called off the judgment. I've also seen the opposite happen—people losing prophesied blessings because of their arrogant behavior.

Prophetic Words Guide
Rather Than Control

Never make a decision based *solely* on the word of a prophet. Prophetic words are meant to support, confirm, or clarify a leading that a person already has or to get that person to pray about a course of action they hadn't thought about. One of my young disciples objected to this restriction. He said, "Well, Isaiah certainly expected people to do what he prophesied."

"That's true, but he was a prophet to kings and nations, and you are not," I replied.

There are different levels of power and scope in all the gifts. The greater gifts give the gifted one greater authority, but no can take the place of God in our lives.

The only person I have personally known who comes close to being a prophet to the nations was John Wimber. More than anyone else in the twentieth century, he changed the way we go to church. Before Wimber, a paid staff did all the ministry of the church. At the conclusion of a service, a minister or two might stand at the front of the church to receive new members. After Wimber, churches all over the world have ministry teams ready to pray for people at the conclusion of the service. No matter where I go in the world, I hear the worship music that Wimber introduced to the church. People sing "I love you" to God in many languages, and now they do it in contemporary music. John had more authority than anyone I've known, but he refrained from controlling people.

When prophets tell people what to do with their money and investments, usually they are perverting the gift of prophecy. The gift of prophecy was given to increase, not our bank accounts, but our love for God and our ability to feel his love for us. I'm not saying that God would never give supernatural guidance to help us manage our finances, but I think that guidance usually comes to us personally in answer to our prayers or through trusted advisers. I also warn prophets not to tell people whom they should marry or whether they should have a baby. This is normally a form of controlling people. One possible exception is the case of a barren couple who wants a child. I have seen a true prophetic word sustain a barren couple with hope and peaceful endurance until the child came.

Translocal Prophets and Teachers

John Paul Jackson had one of the greatest prophetic gifts I've seen. It was appropriate for him to travel to do ministry in other churches and in conferences. But he was always accountable to his home church. I am uncomfortable with prophetic people who aren't anchored in a local church. I feel the same way about translocal teachers.

Prophets and teachers should be raising up new prophets and teachers. Those with a translocal ministry should take disciples with them when possible.

Most of the time, prophets are not good teachers. They should stick to prophetic ministry and raising up other prophetic people. In the same way, most teachers are not good prophets. They should stick to teaching and raising up teachers. Working together, prophets and teachers are a great blessing. They help the leaders of the church create an environment that helps people discover their spiritual gifts and gives them a place to use their gifts.

Deliver Words with
Humility and Kindness

How a prophet shares a word they have for someone also matters. I never let prophets introduce their words with, "Thus saith the Lord," because this implies an infallible authority. I realize that Isaiah, Jeremiah, and Ezekiel all said, "Thus saith the Lord," when they recorded their prophecies, but they were prophets to kings and to nations. When a prophet says, "The Lord tells me . . .," that phrase tends to take away a person's right to question the prophecy. It becomes another form of control. I always encourage prophets to take a humbler route, using a more tentative phrase like, "I think the Lord may be saying . . ."

Similarly, none of us, whether we are prophets or not, should give a critical word to someone unless we have specific permission from the Lord. And then we should do it gently and tactfully (Galatians 6:1). Two pastors whom I did not know came to see me about a problem in their church. I brought a gifted prophet into the meeting. We talked with the pastors for an hour, and then the men left. The prophet did not say a single word. I asked him if he saw anything while we were talking. He said, "Yes, the senior pastor is angry and full of pride. His pride is going to split the church."

"Why didn't you speak up?" I asked.

"Because you told me not to give negative words," he said.

"I did not tell you *not* to give negative words; I told you to give them gently and tactfully," I said.

"Well, how do you tell someone tactfully that their pride is going to split the church?" he asked.

"You say something like this: 'I can tell you really love the church, and you want to do what is right. But some of the people disagree with you. The devil has set a trap for you. He will try to make you so angry with these people that you'll get into a conflict that can't be healed, and good people, people you want and need, will leave the church if you give in to that anger instead of listening patiently to the people who oppose you.'"

"If you frame the warning like that, it will probably be accepted," I said. There is always a tactful way to warn someone.

Whenever we are in doubt, remember that the simple rule for giving prophetic words is to ask God's permission before we give the word. If he says no, obey him. Simple, but it can be so hard to obey when we're certain that what we've seen is true.

When I was a pastor at the Vineyard in Anaheim, a young single mother I hadn't met before came into my office for counseling. She and a man she was dating were serving as Sunday school teachers in our elementary Sunday school. She had come in to talk about a problem with her children, but while she was talking, I had the distinct impression she was sleeping with the man she was dating, but I didn't say anything to her at that time. Later that week, my wife and I happened to be sitting right behind this couple in our Sunday evening service. I leaned over and asked Leesa to pray about this couple to see if God would show her anything about them. They were completely unknown to her. At the end of the service, Leesa said to me, "I don't think that couple is married, but I think they are sleeping together. The man seems to have a lot of religious pride." That was enough for me. I decided to ask them to come into my office for a counseling appointment.

I know we should never accuse people of sin based on our impressions. I had no intention of accusing them. I just wanted to talk to them and gently suggest that I might be able to help with any problems in their relationship. I wanted to give them an opportunity to confess and repent of sin if they really were sleeping together.

Before I called the couple, I prayed, "Lord, do I have your permission to invite them into my office?" I heard an instantaneous "No!" It was not audible or visual. It was an overwhelming feeling that if I tried to bring this couple in for a counseling appointment, I would be displeasing the Lord.

About six weeks later, in a Sunday evening service, John Wimber was preaching on sexual immorality. About two thousand people were present that night. Our Sunday night services were full of visitors who had come to see if the rumors of Vineyard power were true. At the conclusion of his message, John said, "There are a number of you here tonight who are in bondage to sexual immorality." Then he began to list different forms of sexual immorality. Some people were surprised at his frankness, but they were shocked even more at what he did next. John said, "I believe that the Lord is opening a window of grace for you tonight. If you will come forward and publicly confess your sin, and let others pray for you, I believe God will break the power of that evil bondage over many of you."

I had never seen John give an altar call to publicly repent of sexual immorality. I thought perhaps John would call out some other problems, like depression or physical illnesses, and invite those people to come down as well at the same time with the first group. That would afford a little anonymity for those who were in the grip of sexual immorality, and it wouldn't be so embarrassing for them to come down to the front of the church. But John didn't do this. He just stood on the platform and waited for people to respond.

I didn't expect more than five or six people to have the courage to suffer the public humiliation of walking down the aisle to the front of the church to confess their sin. I closed my eyes and began to pray for people to respond to the invitation. I heard lots of chairs move and winter coats hit the floor. Instead of five or six people, more than two hundred people came down to the front of the church to be prayed for. Some may have come to the front because this wasn't their church, and they knew no one would recognize them. But I think most came because John's calm, confidant, nonshaming invitation gave them hope that their bondage would be broken.

So many people were coming down to the altar that there wasn't enough space at the front of the church to contain them. They began to back up into the aisles of the church. Leesa and I were sitting next to the aisle about eight rows back from the front of the church. When Wimber gave the invitation, we stood and prayed with our eyes closed. I could hear people standing, kneeling, and crying in the aisle beside me and behind me. When I opened my eyes and looked down in the aisle to my right, I saw the young couple we had sat behind six weeks earlier, the ones who the Lord had said to Leesa were committing sexual immorality. Leesa and I slipped out of our chairs and knelt down with them.

"Could we pray for you?" I asked.

"I am so ashamed," said the man. "We have been sleeping together and we're not married. We want to get married, but we aren't married yet, and I know it's not right for us to sleep together." Then he added, "I am so filled with pride." We began to pray for them and help them with the process of restoration.

God loved this couple, and he had fixed that day to visit them so they would repent. His way was so much better than my plan to drag a confession out of them. If our ministries are to reach their full potential, we must have the revelatory guidance of the Holy Spirit. We must be able to hear God say a simple no or yes. We must hear the Holy Spirit and not judge by what our eyes see or our ears hear (Isaiah 11:2–4), nor be bound by our traditions (Matthew 15:3).

Be Thankful, Not Critical

Perfectionists are the most miserable people on the planet. Be patient with prophetic ministry. Prophecy was kicked out of the church by bureaucrats in the second and third centuries. Thirty years ago, prophecy began a comeback in the conservative evangelical church in America. Even though we are still basically a one-gift church that teaches almost exclusively and pays a little lip service to evangelism, some churches today do have a full-time prophetic person on staff whose main job is to raise up prophets. Prophecy is messy, and its abuse is destructive. I understand why the apostle Paul had to warn the church not to despise prophecy (1 Thessalonians 5:19–20). But all it took for me was one session with a real prophet who could see the secrets of my heart and the purposes of God for my life to fall in love with prophecy. Once I heard the thunder from the throne, I would never be able to live without the prophets. Before the Lord comes back, I think he will restore prophecy to its rightful place in his church.

Chapter 16

God Speaks in Our

Sufferings

I had only been a Christian for a few months, but I was reading and memorizing Scripture like Jesus was coming back that weekend to test me on my knowledge of his Word. I loved everything I read until I plowed into Philippians 1:29: "It has been granted to you on behalf of Christ not only to believe in him, but also to suffer for him."

I went to church every Sunday morning, every Sunday evening, and every Wednesday evening, and no one had mentioned that suffering was part of the deal. I had given Jesus my life. I was faithfully following Jesus. I wasn't touching the girls or bourbon anymore. I wasn't stealing anymore. Why should I be punished with suffering? Mom never punished me for doing good.

I kept reading, and it got worse. Paul claimed, "I want to know Christ and the power of his resurrection and the fellowship of sharing in his sufferings, becoming like him in his death" (Philippians 3:10 NIV 1984). This verse frightened and repulsed me. It conjured up pictures of a film I had seen in school of these masochistic mystics flagellating their backs into hamburger in some far-off backward country. I was only a baby Christian, yet I still knew better than to call the apostle Paul a masochist. But I could not join Paul in his desire to be crucified. I hoped this suffering thing only applied to the first-century Christians who had been martyred by the Roman government. I lived at a time and under a government where Christians weren't martyred for their faith.

When I had questions about the Bible, I was directed to a woman in our church who was rumored to know the Scripture better than our pastor. She told me to read *The Christian's Secret to a Happy Life* by Hannah Whitall Smith. I didn't need to read the book. The title alone settled the issue for me. What God wanted for his children was a happy life, not a painful life. Follow God and be happy.

I spent almost two decades in seminary as a student and a professor without thinking much about suffering except as a theological obstacle to the existence of a good and omnipotent God. The gift of suffering that Paul promised the Philippians had passed me by. My friends said I lived a charmed life after I had become a Christian. That might have been true until the morning of December 27, 2000, when I found my secondborn son, twenty-two-year-old Scott, dead in his bedroom. He had drunk a lot of alcohol, chased it with a lethal cocktail of drugs, and then shot himself in the head with my .44 Magnum revolver.

For the next ten years, Leesa seemed bent on following Scott out of this world. I followed her into the world of rehabs, emergency room resuscitations, and darker places.

Then just as it seemed we had found "normal" again, Leesa was waylaid by acute respiratory distress syndrome (ARDS) and two massive strokes. She regained the ability to walk, but she had lost her beautiful voice, the sweetest voice I've ever heard. Writing on paper is hard for her. So she ransacks the small vocabulary left in her brain and types words into my phone. I puzzle through the misspellings and convoluted syntax to eventually understand what she is saying.

Every day since June 15, 2013, I have asked God to give back to Leesa what ARDS and the strokes have stolen. Every day, God has said no. Still, I will keep asking as long as the Lord doesn't tell me to stop asking.

For the last twenty years, I have become a student of suffering, not out of a desire to explain its mystery, but so suffering could turn me into a more joyful lover.

I've had pain I did not deserve; I've never had pain I did not need. For none of my pain is random. All of my pain is filtered through God's love for me. My pain is a gift to take me into a deeper place in God, a place I could never have reached without the pain. No loving mother or father would cause their children pain unless it was absolutely necessary for their good. The author of Hebrews tells us to make friends with our pain if we want to be friends with God (Hebrews 12:1–12). He calls pain our trainer (12:11).[1]

---

1. The verb "to train" (*gymnazo*) literally means "to exercise naked" (Walter Bauer, *A Greek–English Lexicon of the New Testament and Other Early Christian Literature*, ed. Frederick W. Danker, 3rd ed. [Chicago: University of

I have worked out with weights in the gym all my life. Just before I turned fifty, I got a trainer who had won bodybuilding contests. That trainer taught me perfect weight lifting form, the order for training the various muscle systems, the proper amount of rest time between training sessions, and how to get the maximum benefit from my cardio workouts. I worked out with that trainer for six years and got into the best shape of my life. I was far stronger in my fifties than I was in my twenties.

When I go to the gym today, I still use the system my trainer taught me. I see so many men lifting in the gym today who don't have a clue what they're doing. Their bodies don't change. They don't get stronger. They are wasting their pain.

Pain is an inevitable fact of life, whether we know God or whether we're still running from him. No one becomes godly without accepting pain as one of our major trainers (1 Timothy 4:7–8). Even though Jesus was the sinless Son of God in his humanity, he learned obedience through his suffering (Hebrews 5:8). It turns out that the greatest friends of God are also the greatest sufferers. They have learned the skill of not wasting their pain (James 1:2–4).

When the Corinthians were in danger of rejecting the apostle Paul and accepting false apostles, Paul appealed to his suffering as one of the main proofs of his apostleship:

Chicago Press, 2000], 208). The Greek word is the source for our word *gym*. There is a sense in which our severe pain strips us naked before our God.

I have worked much harder, been in prison more frequently, been flogged more severely, and been exposed to death again and again. Five times I received from the Jews the forty lashes minus one. Three times I was beaten with rods, once I was pelted with stones, three times I was shipwrecked, I spent a night and a day in the open sea, I have been constantly on the move. I have been in danger from rivers, in danger from bandits, in danger from my fellow Jews, in danger from Gentiles; in danger in the city, in danger in the country, in danger at sea; and in danger from false believers. I have labored and toiled and have often gone without sleep; I have known hunger and thirst and have often gone without food; I have been cold and naked. Besides everything else, I face daily the pressure of my concern for all the churches. Who is weak, and I do not feel weak? Who is led into sin, and I do not inwardly burn?

2 Corinthians 11:23–29

Paul did not waste his pain. Pain is part of the price for consistently moving in the perfected power of God. Every miracle worker is an exceptional sufferer. And this turns out to be a great blessing, for Paul taught that whoever shares in the sufferings of Christ will also share in Christ's glory (Romans 8:17–18).

Paul also knew that suffering for God releases God's power. The cross was the greatest suffering ever endured, and it is still releasing the power of God throughout the world. If we stay with God, we will see him redeem our suffering. He will fill it with meaning and use it to extend his kingdom in a fallen world, giving hope to other sufferers.

Sometimes a friend will ask me, "How did you ever get through that darkness?"

I always say, "The darkness has never been my problem." When I am faced with the loss of what is most precious to me, there is only one Person who can help. I go straight to him. I try not to waste an ounce of my pain.

My problem is prosperity. That's when I drift away from God.

My worst pain has always been unexpected. It comes with a disorienting shock. God is right there at the beginning of the shock, but not in the way I want him to be there. I want to know the purpose of this pain. Everything is spiraling out of its rightful place. I think it would help me if I knew why this blow was necessary. God knows. Only God knows. He knows everything. Unlike me, God is at perfect rest in the citadel of divine simplicity from which he rules everything.[2] Not a single one of his purposes can be thwarted. If I stay with him, eventually he will show me the purpose of my calamity. But at the beginning of the

---

2. I borrowed the phrase "the citadel of divine simplicity" from the brilliant Boethius, the Christian philosopher and statesman who wrote *The Consolation of Philosophy* in AD 524, a magisterial work on the purpose of suffering. The quote is from book 4, section 6, line 25.

bruising, he only says and does the things that will keep me in the fight.

In June 2013, we were visiting friends in Campbellsville, Kentucky. On June 15, I was awakened at 4:30 a.m. by Leesa's gasps for air. A helicopter flew her to the hospital in Louisville. Her lungs had stopped functioning. She came within minutes of dying. She had acute respiratory distress syndrome. ARDS, like irritable bowel syndrome, is a name for a set of symptoms without a precise cause or cure. Ninety percent of the people with ARDS who aren't put on a ventilator die. Fifty percent of the people who *are* put on a ventilator die. They put her on a ventilator in the ICU. The head of pulmonary said, "Get her loved ones here tonight." No one thought she would make it through the night, but she did.

Here's what happened that first week in the ICU.

Each day and night, I sat beside Leesa in her ICU room until they kicked me out. They let me stay until 11:00 p.m., two hours after visiting hours were over. My left hand was on Leesa. I was praying. I had a text list of fifty friends who pray. I texted them the latest updates with my right hand, asking for specific prayers. Each day, Leesa slipped further away. More of her body failed. Our prayers were failing her. I needed a new strategy. I needed more people praying.

I knew that sending out a sterile list of symptoms to pray for wouldn't work.

I decided to write the story of Leesa, me, and God in

the ICU every day. I wouldn't even request prayer. I would listen for God's voice and look for his beauty every day, and then write about it at the close of day, two pages or less. If he didn't show up, I'd write about that. Then I'd post it on Caring Bridge. I called these daily stories "updates." I posted the first one on day 6, Thursday, June 20, 2013.

This is part of the post for day 9, Sunday, June 23, 2013:

Our family has gone home. Our friends from the West and East Coasts have gone home. It is just Leesa and me for the rest of the evening. Leesa is still unconscious. I listen to the rhythmic flow of oxygen, nitric oxide, and air that the ventilator forces down Leesa's lungs. Thirty breaths a minute. No one breathes that fast lying motionless in bed, but the machine forces Leesa to do it in order to keep the level of carbon dioxide down in her blood. I stand on her left side and hold her left hand. I pray for the thousandth time, "Lord, save Leesa." Then I elaborate on that prayer. I break it down into hundreds of parts.

"Lord, heal Leesa's lungs."

"Lord, take the infection out of Leesa's lungs."

"Lord, take fluid out of Leesa's lungs."

Then I go to work on her brain, kidneys, blood, and liver, all of which need fixing.

I speak to evil beings and tell them to let go of Leesa's parts.

I ask the Lord to take Leesa up into heaven and hold her and heal her and show her the mysteries of his glory and then send her back recommissioned for our new life. Those kinds of books where people get sick and are taken up to heaven and sent back are popular now. I want him to write that kind of story for us.

We are coming to the end of our ninth day in this room, and Leesa is still alive and her lungs are making some progress, but not enough to say she is stable, only enough to say she has a chance. I thank God for that progress. Nine days of praying, "Lord, heal Leesa," and monitoring the monitors and talking to nurses and doctors, whose only prognosis is, "She's very, very sick. We'll have to wait and see. This is a day-to-day battle," make me wonder about the power and quality of my prayers. I know prayer works because God says it does. But I see so much impurity in my prayers and feel so little of the passion I think I should have that I wonder how God feels about my prayers. My prayers seem so monotonous to me. I move to the right side of Leesa's bed and hold her right hand, and I've run out of prayers.

I ask God if he will give me another prayer to pray or something to do other than simply standing beside Leesa, holding her hand, wondering where she has gone and if she'll ever come back. Then I hear God say, "You being in the room and loving Leesa and wanting her to be healed is a prayer. You are a prayer. Don't worry about your words. I am listening to the desires of your heart. I am here. I am with you." Then I weep. My first time to cry in Leesa's ICU room. He did not say he would heal her. He said he heard the desire of my heart. He is good, and he always does what is good. I fear that he may think it good for Leesa to finish her race in this ICU bed, and that he may think it good for me to run the rest of my race without her. The one good thing I can say about myself is that I believe with my whole heart that God is good and what he does is good. And for the first time, I can feel him in this room.

It has been years since God came down into that ICU room to give me one of the most glorious affirmations of my life. It is normal for me to be more aware of my failures than my achievements. I don't pray enough. Sometimes it feels like I'm only reciting a shopping list to the Lord before I get on with my real life. Sometimes when I'm thinking the worst of myself, I close my eyes and go back into Leesa's ICU room on June 23, 2013. I take her right hand in mine and feel the despair return. Then I hear God say, "You being in the room and loving Leesa and wanting her to be healed is a prayer. You are a prayer. Don't worry about your words. I am listening to the desires of your heart. I am here. I am with you." And I feel his love all over again. And I feel something else. I feel like the Lord is proud of his little boy, in spite of the boy's poor performance.

We were in Louisville five months before I could bring Leesa home. I continued to write the updates. They were downloaded thousands of times and went all over the world. Networks of churches in Vietnam and other places around the world where I've never been emailed to say they were praying for Leesa every day. People came to Christ and came back to Christ through these updates. People are hungry for stories of experiencing God's love and hearing his voice—even if it's someone else's story. They just want to know it is possible to feel his love and hear him speak. They are comforted to know that none of our suffering is random and that God is always with us to redeem all our pain.

Chapter 17

The Fight

When I was a student at Dallas Seminary, I had the privilege of spending an afternoon with one of our graduates who had become a rock star in the evangelical world. He pastored one of the most famous churches in the country. He told me that when I learned the secret of depending on the Holy Spirit, it would be easier not to sin than to sin. He said you could push a car up a hill, or you could put gas in the car and drive it to the top of the hill. The Holy Spirit is our gas. I believed him, not because he cited convincing scriptural proof, but because I wanted an easier version of the Christian life than the difficult version I was living. He never explained the secret. I guess that's why he called it "the secret." It was something you had to discover on your own. I never found the secret. To this day, it's still pretty easy for me to sin.

I tried other versions of what some called "the higher life." One version practiced in our seminary back then was up-to-the-minute confession of our sin. If we confessed *all* our sin, then we were supposed to be filled with the Holy Spirit. Our version of the filling of the Spirit did not come from the multiple examples in Acts. It was based on a single verse, Ephesians 5:18: "Do not get drunk on wine, which leads to debauchery. Instead, be filled with the Spirit."

Some of our professors said that a person who is drunk is controlled by wine. By contrast a person who is filled with the Spirit is controlled by the Spirit. Every night before I fell asleep, I tried to remember all of my sins so I could confess them and wake up filled with the Spirit. I taught this version of the Christian life to my Young Life kids.

One day, I asked a professor, "If we're controlled by the Spirit, how can we ever sin again?" He said the control was relative. "How relative?" I asked. He did not know. I tossed this useless interpretation of the filling of the Spirit into my theological trash bin. And I enjoyed falling asleep again without thinking about what a horrible person I had been that day.

Then I tried a version of "let go and let God." The idea was that striving is bad news. Striving means you're not depending on God. I tried letting go of my sexual lust, but it wouldn't let go of me. So I let go of this impotent theory of Christian living.

Forever, people have been trying to find a way, a secret, a practice that will make the Christian life easier. Some think that the longer we walk with God, the easier it should be to obey God. But that's not true, not even for Jesus. His greatest struggle came at the end of his life when he sweat drops of blood in Gethsemane (Luke 22:44).

The usual reward for successfully navigating a trial is to

be trusted with a greater trial. I read that in one of the books of The Chronicles of Narnia when I was a young man. It rang true then. I am an old man now, and I can tell you with absolute certainty that it *is* true.

The most popular form of empowered Christian living today involves the baptism of the Holy Spirit. The idea is that we try to live the Christian life by our own power and discipline. This leads us into ever-increasing frustration and disappointment. We call out to God for help again and again, and eventually the Holy Spirit baptizes us with his overwhelming power. Then we have more joy and find it easier to love and obey God. We live on a higher plane than those "unbaptized" Christians. In the Pentecostal version, the evidence that we are baptized by the Spirit is speaking in tongues. And some feel that speaking in tongues gives us a greater access to spiritual power.

The evidence for the Pentecostal version of baptism in the Spirit is found in Acts. The resurrected Jesus tells his apostles that in a few days they will be baptized with the Holy Spirit and power will come on them (Acts 1:5–8). On the day of Pentecost, the Holy Spirit filled the apostles, and they spoke in tongues. Often the filling of the Spirit and baptism of the Spirit are used interchangeably by those who hold this interpretation.

There are many people who will testify that their lives were changed for the good when they began to speak in tongues. I do not doubt the veracity of their testimonies.

Leesa had a supernatural experience when she first spoke in tongues, and the gift has been a blessing to her. What I doubt is that this version of the baptism of the Spirit is a paradigm for all believers. I also doubt any version of the Christian life that seeks to eliminate or minimize significant pain and struggle before we enter heaven.

In the Bible, baptism in the Spirit is not a special empowering given to some Christians to help them live without significant struggles. To be clear, the Holy Spirit does not baptize anyone. John the Baptist said that Jesus baptizes us with the Holy Spirit (Matthew 3:11; Mark 1:8; Luke 3:16). The word *baptize* means "to immerse" or "to dip." Paul wrote, "For in one Spirit we were *all* baptized into one body—Jews or Greeks, slaves or free—and *all* were made to drink of one Spirit" (1 Corinthians 12:13 ESV, emphasis added).[1] When we become Christians, Jesus places us in his body by immersing us in the Holy Spirit. Paul maintains that *all* Christians—not just an elite group pursuing power—have been baptized in the Spirit.

Yet our baptism in the Spirit and the filling of the Spirit are two distinct works. In the book of Acts the filling of the Spirit is a prophetic empowering of a believer to testify that Jesus is the Messiah to unbelievers. It is a repeatable work of the Spirit, in contrast to Jesus baptizing all believers only

---

1. The NIV translates "we were all baptized *by* one Spirit," but the Greek preposition *en* is more normally rendered "in" or "with." And we know that Jesus, not the Spirit, is the one who does the baptizing.

once. In appendix 4, I offer a fuller explanation of the role of the Holy Spirit in the book of Acts and show how the Epistles help to clarify the role of the Holy Spirit.[2]

My point in sharing this is that no single spiritual experience will catapult us into a realm of "easy" Christian living. Revivals and other special times can bring us closer to the Lord. But those times always end, and invariably if we continue to walk with the Lord, we will discover new areas of unbelief and evil in our hearts that we need to surrender to the Lord. There is no example of a person in the New Testament who discovered the secret of an empowered life that exempts a Christian from heartrending struggle.

Although Jesus was perfect in his humanity, he struggled throughout his ministry. He suffered more in his temptation by the devil than anyone else has ever suffered in their testing. Luke tells us that the temptation went on for forty days. Jesus "was led by the Spirit in the wilderness for forty days, being tempted by the devil" (Luke 4:1–2 ESV).[3] The testing was so powerful that Jesus had to fast for forty days. And for those forty days, he felt the full power of Satan's pull to evil—something no one else has ever felt—but he never gave in. It took a toll on him. Angels had to come to help him

---

2. The filling of the Spirit is probably the most misunderstood ministry of the Holy Spirit in the church today. I wrote three chapters (18–20) on the filling of the Spirit in *Why I Am Still Surprised by the Power of the Spirit* (Grand Rapids: Zondervan, 2020), 160–82.

3. "Being tempted" is a present tense participle in Greek, most likely meaning that Jesus was tempted for the whole forty days.

after the devil left (Matthew 4:11). The author of Hebrews claimed that Jesus' suffering during his temptation made him a merciful high priest who could help those in his family who are being tempted by the devil (Hebrews 2:17–18).

Jesus suffered throughout his earthly ministry. The habitual slander, rejection, and plots by the people he loved and came to save hurt him deeply.

> During the days of Jesus' life on earth, he offered up prayers and petitions with fervent cries and tears to the one who could save him from death, and he was heard because of his reverent submission. Son though he was, he learned obedience from what he suffered and, once made perfect, he became the source of eternal salvation for all who obey him.
>
> *Hebrews 5:7–9*

If Jesus required suffering to learn obedience, how much more do we need it?

The cross was Jesus' greatest suffering. It was the greatest act of divine wrath and the greatest act of divine love in human history. Isaiah saw the Son of God and his suffering with a clarity that no other prophet had seen:

> But the LORD was pleased
> To crush Him, putting Him to grief;
> If He would render Himself as a guilt offering,

> He will see His offspring,
>
> He will prolong His days,
>
> And the good pleasure of the LORD will prosper in
> His hand.
>
> *Isaiah 53:10 NASB 1995*

Isaiah doesn't say it was the will of the Lord to crush him; he says it pleased the Lord to crush him.[4] What kind of father would find pleasure in the death of his son? God says he takes no pleasure in the death of a sinner (Ezekiel 18:32), that he doesn't desire anyone to go to hell (2 Peter 3:9), that it is not in his heart to willingly bring affliction or grief to anyone (Lamentations 3:33). But here, the prophet says that God found pleasure in crushing his Son. In what sense did it please the Lord to crush his Son?

The rejection of mankind did not crush the Son of God. The sins of the world did not crush the Son of God. It takes God to crush God. And here is how the Father crushed his Son. God put all the sins of the world on his Son in a way that his Son actually became sin. "God made him who had

---

4. Liberals have always recoiled at the idea that God would punish his innocent Son for the sins of others. Some conservatives who believe in substitutionary atonement recoil at the idea that the Father could delight in the death of his Son. Some of the more recent conservative translations reflect this displeasure by changing "it pleased the LORD to crush his Son" to "it was the will of the LORD to crush his Son." But the verb *chaphets* always means "to take pleasure in, to delight in, to be pleased," and this is exactly how the standard Hebrew lexicons understand the verb (see Brown, Driver, and Briggs [BDB], 856 [2b], https://hebrewcollege.edu/wp-content/uploads/2018/10/BDB.pdf; see also Koehler and Baumgartner [KB], 3rd ed., vol. 1 [3]).

no sin to be sin for us, so that in him we might become the righteousness of God" (2 Corinthians 5:21).

Once the Son shouldered the sin of the world, once all the sins found their mark and came to rest on the heart of the Son of God, the Father abandoned him. He left him all alone, without so much as an apology, not even a goodbye. He put the sin of the world on his Son and then withdrew all help. He forsook him, and for the first time, the Father and the Son were separated. And this is what crushed the Son. His Father left him alone under the weight of the sin of the world. And the Son tells us this from the cross: "My God, my God, why have you forsaken me?" (Matthew 27:46).[5] From noon until three o'clock in the afternoon, the sun did not shine, because for the first and only time, the Light of the world was cut off from his Father and from the Holy Spirit as he bore the sin of the world. The penalty for sin is eternal death. And the Son was able to pay that penalty for all because he is an eternal Person who bore the full brunt of God's wrath for all the sin of the world from the beginning to the end of time.

Imagine a general who sends his son, a captain, into a battle—a battle he knows will take his son's life—but the sacrifice is necessary to win the war. Now imagine the son

---

5. Jesus was not asking for information; he was using a question to express his pain at being forsaken. This is a common figure of speech. Its technical name is *erotesis*, which is simply the Greek word for "questioning." In Scripture there are at least nineteen different uses of *erotesis*. Jesus' use of the question is *erotesis* of lamentation. See E. W. Bullinger, *Figures of Speech Used in the Bible* (1898; repr., Grand Rapids: Baker, 1968), 943–56.

going out at the head of the army to face a larger army. And then just as the conflict begins, the general calls the army back and leaves the captain all alone to fight. Now imagine that the son is facing thousands of soldiers in front of him. He has time to run, but he doesn't. He stands, and he fights. Now they surround him. Still he stands, and he fights. They inflict wound after wound, but the son, who is the captain of the army, won't go down. He stands, he fights, and he bleeds. And he fights all alone. And his wounds hurt, and they weaken him. But no wound hurts like the abandonment of his Father. And yet he still fights on. He fights on until the last enemy soldier falls dead to the ground. Then the Son raises his head and looks out over a battlefield filled with bodies and blood. His wounds are mortal. He has but a few seconds of breath left. He sees no trace of his Father, even though he fought and won the battle for his Father. His Father was not there to witness the Son's victory, and yet the Son calls out to him with his dying breath, "Father, into your hands I commit my spirit." And at last, he falls.

And his Father smiles, and his Father cries. He has never been prouder of his Son. He watched the whole battle, but in a way that kept him hidden from his Son. He abandoned his Son because this was the only way the battle could be won. His Son had to fight alone with no help. And nothing gave the Father more pleasure than watching his Son fight the great fight alone. And nothing gave the Father more pain than watching his Son fight the great fight alone.

People complain about the suffering in this world. But you could take all the human misery in the history of the world and combine it with all the torment of an eternal hell, and it would not equal a drop in the ocean of God's pain on the day the Son of God was crucified.

Jesus said that if we want to be his disciples, we must deny ourselves, take up our cross and follow him (Mark 8:34). Some disciples can do this with joy, but no disciple will do it without a fight.

That is why the apostle Paul called the disciple's life "the good fight" (1 Timothy 1:18; 6:12; 2 Timothy 4:7). No one can be a disciple without striving with all their might against the evil without and the evil within. Paul told the Colossians,

> Him we proclaim, warning everyone and teaching everyone with all wisdom, that we may present everyone mature in Christ. For this I *toil, struggling* with all his energy that he powerfully works within me. For I want you to know how great a *struggle* I have for you and for those at Laodicea and for all who have not seen me face to face.
>
> *Colossians 1:28–2:1 ESV, emphasis added*[6]

---

6. Toiling, struggling, and striving to live as a disciple of Christ are common themes in Paul's ministry and writings (Romans 16:12; 1 Corinthians 9:25; 15:9–10; 16:16; Colossians 4:12; Philippians 2:16; 1 Thessalonians 5:12; 1 Timothy 4:10; 6:12; 2 Timothy 4:7). Paul compares the followers of Jesus to soldiers, athletes, and hardworking farmers, all of whom strive mightily to fulfill their callings (2 Timothy 2:3–6).

None of us can seek the kingdom first without striving, without fighting for all we're worth to fulfill our calling in the kingdom. And when we strive for God's ends, he supplies the power that enables us to fight against the evil that opposes us. As Paul said above, he toiled and struggled "with all his [God's] energy that he powerfully works within me."

God has a trophy room, a hall of fame of faith. He has surrounded us with a great cloud of witnesses, heroes whose weaknesses he turned into strengths so they shut the mouths of lions and walked through flames (Hebrews 11:1–40). In the center of those heroes, stands *the* hero, Jesus, who scorned the shame of the cross and endured its infinite pain that he might present us as a gift to his Father. Anyone who keeps Jesus and his cross at the center of their heart will find the grace to endure their own cross and inherit a place of honor with the heroes of his kingdom.

I stopped looking for the secret of living the Christian life a long time ago. There is no secret. God has never tried to hide the cross. He has never tried to hide the pain of the cross. The older I grow, the more I feel the pain of my cross.

On December 18, 1965, when I prayed my first prayer, a single sentence in the middle of the night—"Lord, I'm comin' over to your side"—I did not know that Jesus wanted to be my friend and that he wanted to give me a crown so he could brag on me for all eternity. All I did that night was say yes to his offer of eternal life. He had spoken to me.

How else would I have known I could come over to his side and that he would never leave me? He never stopped speaking to me. That's just what fathers do. For a little while, I believed in the voice. But then I got smart and outgrew my need to hear my Father's voice. He just smiled at his little boy. That's what the great fathers do. I kept right on growing prouder of my knowledge of his written Word. I used the skills he gave me to distance myself from him. "For though the LORD is high, he regards the *lowly*, but the haughty he knows from afar" (Psalm 138:6 ESV, emphasis added). I taught the Psalms in Hebrew, but that verse never found a home in my heart until I heard the voice of the Lord speaking to me outside of the Bible.

I began my journey to "the lowly" on a stage with a depressed woman and a demon. In spite of all my scriptural and theological knowledge, I had no power to help the woman and no power over the demon. The voice broke through all my theological defenses and explained my powerlessness. "You are a deceiver and manipulator, and you're just playing at church," the voice said. My quest to hear the voice was birthed at that moment.

I can't imagine how I could have ever become a friend of God without hearing his voice often. How can we be friends with anyone unless we hear their voice frequently? When I began my walk with Christ, I had no idea of the suffering that lay in store for me. The Lord delayed the worst of the suffering until I had learned to hear my Father's voice. Without the voice, my enemy would have waylaid me with trauma. Instead, the voice used my disasters to draw me deeper into the abyss of divine love.

The voice has brought me around to Paul's way of thinking: "I want to know Christ and the power of his resurrection and the fellowship of sharing in his sufferings, becoming like him in his death" (Philippians 3:10 NIV 1984). Paul spoke for all the friends of Jesus. The heart of the Son of God is so big that his reward for our temporal suffering is an eternal commendation that we will wear as a crown forever: "Well done, good and faithful servant! You have been faithful with a few things; I will put you in charge of many things. Come and share your master's happiness!" (Matthew 25:21). Those words of praise will echo forever throughout eternity. A few years of struggling to overcome evil can give us an eternal place of honor alongside the Son of God on his throne (Revelation 3:21).

If my only resources were my knowledge of Scripture and my personal discipline, I would never have a shot at that eternal crown, and I would have forfeited so much joy during my earthly days. Like Jesus, I need to hear my Father's voice to fulfill my highest purposes and bring my Father joy. The wisdom of God is amazing. He gives us a friendship in which he makes himself and us happy when we hear the voice of Jesus.

Supernatural Ministry in
Every Chapter of Acts

Chapter 1. After his resurrection, Jesus appeared to the eleven apostles (vv. 3–9). After Jesus ascended into heaven, angels came down and gave the Eleven directions (vv. 10–11).

Chapter 2. A violent wind and tongues of fire swept in the room where the 120 were praying, and they all spoke in tongues (vv. 2–4). Then Peter preached an inspired sermon, quoting the promise of prophetic ministry from Joel 2:28–32 (vv. 14–36).

Chapter 3. The healing of the man lame from birth at the temple gate called Beautiful revealed the glory of Christ (v. 13).

Chapter 4. Peter's defense of the gospel and the apostles' ministry was an example of the filling of Holy Spirit (supernatural prophetic testimony to Jesus) and a fulfillment of Jesus' own prophecy in Luke 12:11–12 and 21:12–15 (vv. 8–12).

Chapter 5. Peter prophesied the death of Ananias and Sapphira (vv. 3–11). An angel freed the apostles from jail (vv. 19–20).

Chapter 6. Stephen performed miraculous signs and wonders and spoke so effectively by the Holy Spirit that no one could refute him (vv. 8, 10).

Chapter 7. In Stephen's final moments, the Lord Jesus revealed himself to Stephen so that he could see the Son of God standing at the right hand of the Father (v. 55).

Chapter 8. An angel from heaven gave directions to Philip for ministry (v. 26), and then the Holy Spirit spoke to him directly, giving him further directions (v. 29). Finally, the Spirit himself carried Philip away to Azotus (v. 39).

Chapter 9. Jesus appeared to Saul and gave him the beginning of his commission on the Damascus road (vv. 3–6). Jesus spoke to Ananias and sent him to minister to Saul (vv. 10–16).

Chapter 10. An angel appeared in a vision to Cornelius and told him to send for Peter (vv. 4–6). In the meantime, God caused Peter to fall into a trance, gave him a vision, and declared to him that all foods were clean (vv. 10–16). The Holy Spirit spoke to Peter and told him to go with the three men Cornelius had sent (vv. 19–20). While Peter was preaching to Cornelius, the Holy Spirit fell on Cornelius and all the Gentiles in his house so that all of them spoke in tongues (v. 46).

Chapter 11. The prophet Agabus correctly predicted a famine (v. 28).

Chapter 12. An angel visited Peter in his jail cell and delivered him from certain death (vv. 7–11).

Chapter 13. The Holy Spirit spoke to the church at Antioch, telling them to set apart Barnabas and Saul for a specific ministry (v. 2). On his first missionary journey, Paul accurately predicted a judgment against the sorcerer Elymas so that Elymas was blinded (vv. 9–12).

Chapter 14. While Paul was preaching at Lystra, a man was sitting in the audience who had been lame from birth. Paul looked at him while he spoke and supernaturally saw that the man had faith to be healed. Paul told the man to stand up, and he was instantly healed (vv. 9–10).

Chapter 15. The Holy Spirit communicated to the apostles and elders in the Jerusalem council that it was good not to burden the Gentiles with the law (v. 28).

Chapter 16. On Paul's second missionary journey, the Holy Spirit forbade Paul and his companions to preach the gospel in Asia (v. 6). The Holy Spirit also denied Paul and his companions permission to enter Bithynia (v. 7). At Troas, Paul was given a vision of a man in Macedonia, urging them to come over and help (vv. 9–10). This proved to be the direction in which the Lord was leading Paul's missionary team. At Philippi the Lord specifically opened Lydia's heart to believe the gospel that Paul was preaching (v. 14).

Chapter 17. Many of the Berean Jews and prominent Greeks believed in Jesus (v. 12), and a few members of the Areopagus believed as well (v. 34).

Chapter 18. The Lord spoke to Paul in a night vision

and told him that no one would harm him and that the Lord had many people in the city of Corinth (vv. 9–11).

Chapter 19. Twelve believers at Ephesus on whom Paul laid his hands spoke in tongues and prophesied (v. 6). Paul did extraordinary miracles in Ephesus (v. 11).

Chapter 20. Paul raised Eutychus from the dead at Troas (v. 10). At Miletus, Paul told the Ephesian elders he was compelled by the Spirit to go to Jerusalem (v. 22). He also said the Holy Spirit had warned him that suffering was waiting for him (v. 23). Paul also prophesied that the Ephesian elders would never see him again (v. 25) and that after he left, savage wolves would attack the Ephesian church.

Chapter 21. A number of believers urged Paul through the Spirit not to go to Jerusalem because they knew of the danger waiting for him there (v. 4). This chapter also records that Philip's four daughters were all prophetesses (v. 9). Agabus prophesied to Paul that the Jews of Jerusalem would bind Paul and hand him over to the Gentiles (vv. 10–11).

Chapter 22. Paul retold the story of his conversion and how the Lord appeared to him on the Damascus road (vv. 6–16). He also told about falling into a trance while in the temple and how the Lord warned him to leave Jerusalem and revealed he was sending him to the Gentiles (vv. 17–21).

Chapter 23. The Lord appeared to Paul while he was held prisoner in Jerusalem, telling him he would testify about Jesus not only in Jerusalem but also in Rome (v. 11).

Chapter 24. In Caesarea, Paul gave a speech before Felix, the governor, that was inspired by the Holy Spirit in fulfillment of Luke 12:11–12 and 21:12–15 (vv. 10–21).

Chapter 25. Paul gave another speech at Caesarea to Festus, the governor who succeeded Felix, that must be viewed in the same light as the speech of chapter 24—an inspired utterance by the Holy Spirit in fulfillment of Luke 12:11–12 and 21:12–15 (vv. 8–12).

Chapter 26. When King Agrippa came to visit Paul, he retold the story again of his conversion and how the Lord had appeared to him on the Damascus road (vv. 9–16).

Chapter 27. Paul accurately predicted the destruction of the ship meant to take him to Rome (v. 10). An angel of the Lord appeared to him during the night, telling him he would not drown in the shipwreck and that God would spare the lives of all who were on board with him (vv. 21–26).

Chapter 28. In the final chapter, a miracle occurred when a poisonous viper bit Paul's hand, but he was not hurt (vv. 3–6). This led to a series of miracles in which Paul was the instrument for the healing of all the sick on the island of Malta (vv. 7–9).

Appendix 2

Supernatural Ministry
Is Normal for Christians
in the New Testament

Cessationists argue that God permitted the apostles to do supernatural ministry to show that they were trustworthy teachers of doctrine. They claim that since we have their doctrine in the completed New Testament, there is no longer a need for supernatural ministry. This argument contains at least four methodological errors.

The first error is that no scriptural text teaches that the purpose of miracles was to authenticate the apostles as trustworthy teachers of doctrine. Scripture states at least ten divine purposes for miracles. These purposes are rooted in the eternal character of God, not in the historical transition from Old Testament worship to New Testament worship.[1]

The second error is the failure to distinguish the ministry of signs and wonders, which is an extraordinary outpouring of miracles in times of revival led by the few, from the Holy Spirit's distribution of spiritual gifts to the whole body of Christ at all times.

---

1. For a detailed discussion of the purposes of New Testament healing and miracles, see my *Why I Am Still Surprised by the Power of the Spirit* (Grand Rapids: Zondervan, 2020), 106–15.

The third error is the failure to explain why two who were not apostles, Stephen and Philip, did signs and wonders. This is an insurmountable exception to the theory that the purpose of signs and wonders was to authenticate the apostles as trustworthy teachers of doctrine. Cessationists reply that Stephen and Philip were able to do signs and wonders because the apostles laid hands on them. This simply begs the question. If the purpose of signs and wonders was to authenticate the apostles as trustworthy teachers of doctrine, there is absolutely no reason that Stephen and Philip should have done signs and wonders.[2]

The fourth error is that the cessationist argument is bad and inconsistent theology. The authority of Scripture does not rest on the miraculous ministry of apostles, but on God, the ultimate author of Scripture. Only three of the original twelve wrote Scripture. The gospels of Mark and Luke and the book of Acts were not written by apostles. Are these books less "trustworthy" then?

The fifth error involves misunderstanding the character of narrative literature and basing a doctrine on an argument from silence. In each instance, when the book of Acts uses the expression "signs and wonders," it refers to an *abundance* of miracles done by those who are preaching Jesus.

---

2. The book of Acts does not mention any miraculous powers given to the other five men on whom the apostles laid hands. According to Acts 6:1–6, the purpose of the laying on of hands was not to impart miraculous powers but to set aside these seven men to take charge of the food ministry and make sure that all were treated fairly.

Who engages in a ministry of signs and wonders in the book of Acts? Luke tells us twice that the apostles were doing "many signs and wonders" (Acts 2:43; 5:12). When he gives us specific illustrations of apostolic miracles, he only shows us miracles worked through Peter or Paul. The only other specific examples of a ministry of signs and wonders are the ministries of Stephen and Philip.

The fact that only the apostles Stephen and Philip appear in Acts doing signs and wonders does not mean no one else in New Testament times or subsequent times would not be given a ministry of signs and wonders. The narrative literature of the Bible only tells the story of the few. The book of Acts, for example, has Peter as its main character in the first twelve chapters, with a small role played by John and somewhat larger roles played by Stephen and Philip. From chapter 13 to the end of the book, Paul is the dominant character. The narrative literature of the Bible is *the story of special people*—people who play significant roles in God's redemptive history. The overwhelming majority of biblical examples of both godly ministry and passionate devotion are drawn from the lives of the few, special, and exceptional characters who became prominent in salvation history. It is impossible, therefore, to justify logically or biblically a hermeneutical principle that (1) is *primarily based* on the *observation* that only a few in the Bible possess or do certain things, and (2) functions to justify the cessation of these things.

Paul is the only significant church planter in the New Testament, and most of the apostles seem to stay in Jerusalem rather than going out to plant churches. Does that mean that only the few were intended to plant churches, and that when Paul died, church planting also died? Even though the observation is correct, the conclusion is false, because it contradicts New Testament commands to evangelize and disciple the world (Matthew 28:18–20; Luke 24:47; Acts 1:8). The fact that only a few possess or do certain things, therefore, is irrelevant *in itself* to determine whether such things were meant to be temporary or permanent in the life of the church.

Scripture presents the lives of special people to Christian readers as examples to copy (1 Corinthians 4:16–17; 11:1; Philippians 3:17; 4:9; 1 Thessalonians 1:6; Hebrews 11:4–12:3). Modern interpreters, however, who have no experience of the miraculous, assume an antisupernatural method of interpretation at this point. They read the stories of the apostles, Stephen, Philip, Agabus, and others in the book of Acts and assume that the divine guidance and miracles associated with their lives are not to be copied or even hoped for in the modern Christian experience. On a theoretical level, this assumption may or may not be true, but for it to carry conviction, it needs to be based on clear statements of Scripture, not simply on the observation that only a few people did miracles in the New Testament.

The following survey shows a wide distribution of supernatural ministry in the New Testament.

Jesus granted authority to the *seventy-two* to heal the sick in their preaching mission (Luke 10:9). They returned with joy, saying, "Lord, even the demons submit to us in your name" (10:17). This is a tremendous exception to the theory that only a few received miraculous gifts, and then only for the purpose of authenticating the apostles.

There was also the anonymous man who was the subject of the interchange between John and Jesus in Mark 9:38–39:

> "Teacher," said John, "we saw someone driving out demons in your name and we told him to stop, because he was not one of us."
>
> "Do not stop him," Jesus said. "For no one who does a miracle in my name can in the next moment say anything bad about me."

This is an extremely interesting case. Here we have an anonymous man in the Gospels who was doing something that only Jesus and the apostles had been empowered to do—namely, drive out demons. Yet neither Jesus nor the apostles had laid hands on this man and recognized him as an official member of the apostolic band. Even in the Gospels, the ministry of the miraculous was not limited to the twelve apostles, nor was it distinctively for their authentication.

When we turn to the book of Acts, we discover that many people exercised various miraculous gifts of the Holy Spirit. There were many people who spoke in tongues:

1. The one hundred and twenty (Acts 1:15; 2:1–4).
2. The Samaritans (they almost certainly spoke in tongues, for Acts 8:18 tells us that Simon "saw" the Samaritans receiving the Holy Spirit).
3. Cornelius and the Gentiles with him (Acts 10:45–46).
4. The twelve disciples at Ephesus (Acts 19:6).

A number of people are mentioned in Acts who had received the gift of prophecy:

1. The prophet Agabus (Acts 11:28; 21:10–11).
2. The individuals in Acts 13:1.
3. Prophets Judas and Silas (Acts 15:32).
4. The disciples at Tyre who "through the Spirit . . . urged Paul not to go on to Jerusalem" (Acts 21:4).
5. Philip's four unmarried daughters who prophesied (Acts 21:9).
6. Ananias (Acts 9:10–18).

When Stephen and Philip are added to the list just mentioned, an impressive variety of nonapostolic figures received and exercised miraculous charismata in a book that is almost exclusively devoted to the ministries of Peter and Paul.

Ananias is one of the more interesting examples of a nonapostolic character who has a miraculous ministry. His relative obscurity makes him all the more interesting. The only thing we know about him is that he was "a devout observer of the law and highly respected by all the Jews living there" (Acts 22:12). In Ananias's ministry to Saul, he exercised both a healing gift and a prophetic gift (9:10–18). But more than this, it was at the hands of Ananias that Saul was filled with the Holy Spirit (9:17). God used Ananias, not an apostle, to confer the Holy Spirit to an apostle. It is likely that the apostle Paul was given his miracle-working powers at this very instance, because he not only received the Holy Spirit at this time but was also to be *filled with the Holy Spirit* when Ananias laid hands on him (9:17).[3]

In the book of Acts, we find so many exceptions to the idea that only a few received supernatural gifts and that the supernatural gifts were exclusively for the authentication of the apostles that we are forced to abandon this theory.

The evidence from the rest of the New Testament is even more devastating to cessationist theory. All of the gifts of the Spirit were in operation at the church in Corinth (1 Corinthians 12:7–10). Some have argued that 1 Corinthians 12:8–10 contains a summary of the gifts

---

3. For a detailed explanation of what it means to be filled with the Spirit, see *Why I Am Still Surprised*, 160–82.

given to the whole church rather than gifts that were actually present in the Corinthian church. Their goal is to suggest that only the apostles and a few others experienced the miraculous gifts. They would like us to believe that the average Corinthian Christian only had the "nonmiraculous" gifts.[4] Paul specifically contradicts this suggestion when he tells the Corinthians that none of the spiritual gifts (*charismata*) were lacking among them (1 Corinthians 1:7). The description in 1 Corinthians 14:26, where tongues and prophecy were present in the normal Corinthian worship service, also contradicts this interpretation. The gift of prophecy was also in use in Rome (Romans 12:6), Ephesus (Ephesians 4:11), and Thessalonica (1 Thessalonians 5:20). The casual way in which Paul mentions miracles in Galatians 3:5 suggests that miracles were common among the Galatian churches.

The New Testament church was a miracle-working church. And this is exactly what we should expect from the body of Christ.

---

4. There is no such thing as a nonmiraculous gift of the Spirit. All of the gifts are given by the Holy Spirit and require his power and guidance to be effectively used. The gift of teaching is just as miraculous as the gift of healing. The Holy Spirit reveals the excellencies of the Trinity to the teacher and then empowers the teacher to use that revelation to heal and change the human heart which is "beyond cure" without supernatural power (Jeremiah 17:9–10).

Deuteronomy
18:14–22

Deuteronomy 18:14–22 is frequently understood by cessationists who betray no knowledge of the scholarly exegesis on the passage as referring to a succession of prophets from Moses onward who would never make a mistake in their predictions. Several contextual factors argue against this interpretation. First, Moses did not say that God would raise up a line of prophets, but rather *a prophet* (v. 15). Second, Moses claimed that this future prophet would be *like him* (v. 15). Moses was not simply a prophet who foretold the future; he was the theocratic founder of Israel's religion and the mediator of the old covenant. The qualifying phrase "like me" means that the prophet who is to come will also be a covenant mediator. Third, the epilogue to Deuteronomy, which was written in the time of Joshua or later, specifically states:

> Since then, no prophet has risen in Israel like Moses, whom the LORD knew face to face, who did all those signs and wonders the LORD sent him to do in Egypt—to Pharaoh and to all his officials and to his whole land. For no one has ever shown the mighty power

or performed the awesome deeds that Moses did in the sight of all Israel.

Deuteronomy 34:10–12

This means that not even Joshua was on a par with Moses, even though God promised to be with him, just as he had been with Moses (Joshua 1:5). The significance of Deuteronomy 34:10–12, according to Patrick Miller, is that "one can hardly see 18:15–22 in terms of a continuing line of prophets through Israel's history. The only way to resolve the tension between chapters 18 and 34 is to project *into the future* the announcement that God will raise up a prophet."[1] Fourth, this was how the passage was interpreted in Judaism.[2] Fifth, in the New Testament, both the Jews and the apostles understood this passage to refer not to a line of prophets but to the Messiah (John 1:21, 25; 6:14; 7:40; Acts 3:22–26). Therefore, the context and later biblical interpretation demonstrate that the messianic interpretation of Deuteronomy 18:14–22 is the correct interpretation.

Deuteronomy 18:14 sets the context against the background of sorcery and divination in the land of Canaan, which Israel is about to possess. The false prophets mentioned in 18:20–22 are not prophets who simply make a

---

1. Patrick Miller, *Deuteronomy* (Louisville, KY: Westminster John Knox, 1990), 155–56, emphasis in original.
2. See Peter C. Craigie, *The Book of Deuteronomy* (Grand Rapids: Eerdmans, 1976), 263 n20.

mistake, but rather pretenders to the place of Moses or to the messianic role attempting to lead Israel to false gods. Craigie supports this interpretation of 18:20–22:

> It would probably be wrong to take these criteria as rules to be applied rigidly every time a prophet opened his mouth. When a prophet announced God's coming judgment and called for repentance, it would clearly be pointless to wait first to see if the judgment actually came to pass, and then to repent (too late!). Rather the criteria represent the means by which a prophet gained his reputation as a true prophet and spokesman of the Lord. Over the course of a prophet's ministry, in matters important and less significant, the character of a prophet as a true spokesman of God would begin to emerge clearly. And equally, false prophets would be discredited and then dealt with under the law.[3]

Furthermore, there is no evidence in Israel's history that they ever put to death a prophet for a simple mistake in a prophetic utterance. For example, when David implied to Nathan that he wanted to build a temple for the Lord, Nathan said to him, "Whatever you have in mind, go ahead and do it, for the LORD is with you" (2 Samuel 7:3). But Nathan was wrong and later that night had to be corrected

---

3. Craigie, *Book of Deuteronomy*, 263.

by the Lord (7:4–17). If someone pedantically objects that Nathan did not preface his first prophecy with "Thus says the LORD . . . ," it should be noted that Nathan did speak in the name of the Lord, for he said, "the LORD is with you." Besides, would David have spoken to Nathan simply to obtain the prophet's human opinion? Why did people consult prophets in the Old Testament if not to receive a word from God? Nathan gave a wrong word, but he was not put to death. A wrong word was not automatically classified as a presumptuous word or a word in the name of false gods (Deuteronomy 18:20–22).

I believe that Scripture is inerrant. Anything that a teacher, wise man, psalmist, prophet, or an apostle writes in Scripture will be inerrant. Apart from the writing of Scripture, all teachers, prophets, and even apostles make mistakes. Paul publicly rebuked Peter for compromising the gospel at Antioch. Peter was eating with Gentiles at Antioch. But when James sent Jewish Christians from Jerusalem, Peter stopped eating with the Gentiles. Even Barnabas was carried away by Peter's hypocrisy (Galatians 2:11–21). Only Jesus was perfect in ministry.

The Ministry of the Holy Spirit and the Book of Acts

I. Some of the Various Ministries of the Holy Spirit

   A. The Holy Spirit regenerates—causes the rebirth of—those who believe in Christ.

      1. John 3:3–7 (born again).

      2. Titus 3:5: "He saved us, not because of righteous things we had done, but because of his mercy. He saved us through the washing of rebirth and renewal by the Holy Spirit."

      3. 2 Corinthians 5:17 tells us that since we are born again, we have a new nature.

   B. The Holy Spirit indwells all believers.

      1. 1 Corinthians 6:19: "Do you not know that your bodies are temples of the Holy Spirit, who is in you, whom you have received from God?"

      2. Romans 8:9: "You, however, are not in the realm of the flesh but are in the realm of the Spirit, if indeed the Spirit of God lives in you. And if anyone does not have the Spirit of Christ, they do not belong to Christ."

      3. In the Old Testament, the only person assured of the presence of the Spirit was the king. But

even here the thought is that the Spirit "came powerfully upon David" (1 Samuel 16:13) and is with the king rather than the Spirit indwelling the king.

    4. The Spirit could not be given to indwell believers until Jesus had been crucified and then glorified (John 7:37–39).

C. At the moment of our new birth, we are sealed by the Spirit. The Holy Spirit is the seal guaranteeing that we are owned by God and that we will be taken to heaven at the end of our earthly lives.

    1. 2 Corinthians 1:22.

    2. Ephesians 1:13.

    3. Ephesians 4:30.

D. The Holy Spirit gives all believers spiritual gifts.

    1. 1 Corinthians 12:11.

    2. There are twenty-one spiritual gifts.[1]

E. The Holy Spirit fills believers. This means the Spirit supernaturally empowers believers to give prophetic testimony that Jesus is the Messiah.

    1. In Luke, the filling of the Spirit is a onetime event empowering Zechariah, Elizabeth, and John to testify to Jesus as the Messiah before Jesus was born.

---

1. See Jack Deere, *Why I Am Still Surprised by the Power of the Spirit* (Grand Rapids: Zondervan, 2020), 253–78.

2. This is not a onetime empowering meant to help us live the Christian life better, but in Acts it is a repeatable empowering to help us evangelize. In Acts, unbelievers are present every time someone is filled with the Spirit.

3. The first people filled with the Spirit are Elizabeth (Luke 1:41), John as a baby in Elizabeth's womb (Luke 1:14, with 1:41), and Zechariah at John's birth (Luke 1:67). All of these are a prophetic empowering testifying to John's role as the forerunner of the Messiah.

4. These are the evangelistic examples of prophetic empowering: Acts 2:4; 4:8, 31; 9:17; 13:9.[2]

F. The Holy Spirit leads and guides believers.

1. Romans 8:14.

2. Acts 16:6–10.

G. The Holy Spirit reveals the excellencies of the Trinity and teaches believers about Jesus and his kingdom.

1. John 14:15–17, 26.

2. John 15:26.

3. John 16:12–15.

H. The Holy Spirit intercedes for all believers: Romans 8:26–27.

I. The Holy Spirit testifies to Christians' spirits that we are children of God: Romans 8:16.

---

2. For a full explanation of the filling of the Spirit, see *Why I Am Still Surprised by the Power of the Spirit*, 160–82.

J. The Holy Spirit inspired the prophets and writers of Scripture.

    1. The prophets searched their own written prophecies to understand the messianic times and circumstances that the Spirit of Christ was predicting through them (1 Peter 1:10–12).

    2. The Old Testament prophets "were carried along by the Holy Spirit" (2 Peter 1:21).

    3. David, the author of many psalms, claims, "The Spirit of the LORD spoke through me" (2 Samuel 23:2).

II. Baptism *in* the Spirit, not *by* the Spirit.

  A. Jesus baptizes every believer in the Holy Spirit. The Spirit is not the baptizer. John the Baptist said, "He [Jesus] will baptize you with the Holy Spirit" (Matthew 3:11).

  B. The Greek verb *baptizo* ("baptize") means "to dip or immerse." The first English translators of the New Testament did not translate the verb; they merely transliterated it into English letters. Jesus immerses every believer into the Spirit the moment they believe in him. This is how Jesus places us into his body.

    1. "For *in* one Spirit we were all baptized into one body" (1 Corinthians 12:13 ESV, emphasis added).

    2. The translation found in the older translations— "we were all baptized *by* one Spirit"—is surely

wrong. John the Baptist said that *Jesus* is the baptizer. The Greek preposition *en* usually means "in" or "with," not "by." If Paul had wanted to make it clear that the Spirit was doing the baptizing, he would have used the preposition *hypo*. When we believe in Jesus, he immerses us in the Spirit, and this act places us in his body.

3. All Christians are baptized in the Spirit (1 Corinthians 12:13).

III. The confusion over "baptism in the Spirit" results from misunderstanding the stories of Acts.

A. In Acts 2, the Spirit regenerates, indwells, seals, gives spiritual gifts, and fills the 120. But Luke only mentions two of these works: the filling of the Spirit and the giving of the gift of tongues.

B. Jesus said to the disciples before Pentecost, "In a few days you will be baptized with [or in] the Holy Spirit" (Acts 1:5). This has led some people to think that everything that happened in Acts 2 is the baptism by the Spirit. They think that the filling of the Spirit and baptism in the Spirit are the same thing and that speaking in tongues is the evidence of baptism by the Spirit. They think that baptism in the Spirit is what gives us power to live a "victorious" life. Since the 120 were already believers, these people think that baptism in the Spirit happens after we've been believers for a while and have finally come to realize how much we need supernatural help to live the Christian life.

C. This mistaken interpretation comes from failing to interpret the stories of Acts in light of the other biblical statements about the baptism with the Spirit, notably that Jesus is the baptizer, not the Spirit, and that all Christians are baptized in the Spirit and this act places them in the body of Christ rather than empowering them to live a successful Christian life.

Acknowledgments

Michael Rowntree and Michael Miller had just graduated from college when they first came to my church. They were already disciples of Jesus who were focused on being friends with the Lord, leading young people to Christ, and turning them into disciples. They were smart and witty. Hanging out with them was a total pleasure. I taught them how to do prophetic ministry and healing. They excelled at both, and I began to take them to my conferences to do ministry. We have been around the world together, and both are in demand as conference speakers. Michael Rowntree pastors Bridgeway Church in Oklahoma City and can be heard regularly on the popular *Remnant Radio* podcast. Michael Miller pastors Reclamation Church in Denver and is a frequent guest on the *Remnant Radio* podcast. The stories of healings and prophetic words from their ministries included in *Why I Am Still Surprised by the Voice of God* have made it a better book than I could have written on my own. My friendship with these two is one of the great gifts that God has given to me.

Why I Am Still Surprised by the Power of the Spirit

Discovering How God Speaks and Heals Today

Jack Deere

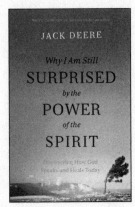

When Jack Deere turned seventeen, he did not know God or a single verse of Scripture. At twenty-seven, he became a professor at Dallas Theological Seminary. He started and pastored an influential church in Fort Worth, Texas. He taught his church and his students that God no longer gave the "miraculous gifts of the Spirit" or spoke outside the pages of Scripture.

After Deere had taught for ten years, a bestselling author shocked him when he told him he not only believed God was regularly healing people today, but that he had seen undeniable miracles in answer to his prayers. For the next four months, Deere studied every healing story in the New Testament and became convinced, against his will, that God was still healing and speaking, just as he had done in the New Testament.

In *Why I Am Still Surprised by the Power of the Spirit*, Deere tells documented stories of modern miracles. He explains the nature of spiritual gifts, defines each spiritual gift, offers sound advice on discovering and using the gifts today, and shows how all of this part of God's way of deepening our friendship with him.

The modern classic *Surprised by the Power of the Spirit* was published twenty-five years ago, and in that book Deere claimed he would live long enough to see the majority of conservative evangelicals come to believe in all the gifts of the Spirit. That has come true. The theological landscape has changed dramatically. This new edition contains about 70 percent new material on the practical matters of experiencing and using spiritual gifts. Deere shares many new stories of God's power and introduces the latest literature defending and explaining the gifts of the Spirit. All this and more will continue the book's legacy for a new generation.

Even in Our Darkness

A Story of Beauty in a Broken Life

Jack Deere

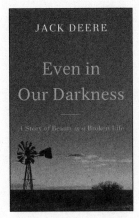

> *"Filled with the raw pain, beauty, mystery, and grace that our hearts were meant for."*
> Matt Chandler

Prepare yourself for an unvarnished look at the Christian life, told now for the first time. A powerful memoir of finding beauty and friendship through the pain of loss, tragedy, and brokenness, *Even in Our Darkness* explores what it means to know God and be known by him.

Jack Deere tells the true story of his life growing up near Fort Worth, Texas, in the 1950s and the disintegration of his family following his father's suicide. In his mid-twenties, Jack would rise to fame and success as a leading scholar, popular speaker, and bestselling author.

But despite being rescued and exalted, Jack would ultimately be crushed in the years that followed. He would lose his son to suicide and his wife to alcoholism. Only then would Jack wrestle with his own addictions, surrender control, and experience true healing.

An authentic story of the Christian life, *Even in Our Darkness* will serve as your own guide in overcoming life's disappointments and learning to hear God speak in unbelievable ways.

Available in stores and online!